# Anna Hinderer

## Pioneer Missionary

From the tranquillity of Victorian East Anglia to the turmoil of Ibadan, West Africa

Ann Meakin

Connaught Books

First published in Great Britain in 2015 by Connaught Books



British Library Cataloguing in Publication Data

A catalogue record for this book is available from the British Library
ISBN 978-0-9557454-3-0

Printed in England by the Lavenham Press Ltd.

Every effort has been made to contact copyright holders and obtain relevant permissions.

For Chris, Michael and Neville

without whose help this book would never have reached publication

# CONTENTS

# ACKNOWLEDGMENTS

This book could not have been produced without the help of a great many people.

First and foremost I would like to thank the Robarts Library of the University of Toronto for putting online the book 'Seventeen Years In The Yoruba Country'. That book was my inspiration. My quotations from Anna's letters, her journal and her drawings have been copied from it.

Also I would particularly like to thank the following:-
The Right Reverend Graham James, Lord Bishop of Norwich, for his encouragement and for his very thoughtful foreword.
Professor Neville Skinner, formerly of Ibadan University shared with me his extensive knowledge of Lowestoft and escorted me around the parts associated with Anna. He also did a great deal of genealogical research to find Anna's relatives and create her family tree. He edited my first draft of this book.
Christopher J. Harrison spent a great deal of time making the illustrations presentable and solving my many computer problems.
Dr Michael Vickers, formerly of Ife University, Nigeria, came into my life at a very crucial time, when I needed to be jolted into renewed action. His help in explaining the intricacies of the history of Nigeria and his interest and encouragement have been invaluable.
C. John Cotton provided me with the information about the ships plying between England and West Africa.
Mrs Dolapo Falomo provided the photograph of the house built by the Hinderers at Kudeti, Ibadan.
Liverpool History Society provided information about Mr and Mrs Mather of Bootle Hall.
Peter Boon provided information about the Mutford and Lothingland Workhouse.
N. W. (Bill) Bracey did the final proof reading.

Michael Blackwell of Connaught Books patiently guided me to publication.
Many other people have answered my questions and made suggestions for research and these include, The Revd. Jack Burton, Dr. Mary Fewster, Dr. Nicholas Groves, Pamela Minett, Roy Tricker, Norma Virgoe, the people at Norwich Cathedral Library, and the staff at Lowestoft and Norwich Record Offices.
Final thanks must be given to our daughter Rachel who helped with her expertise in presentation and my husband John for doing rather more than his share of the household tasks while I worked on this project.

The proceeds from the sales of this book will be donated to the Church Mission Society (formerly the Church Missionary Society).

Ann Meakin
Martham
2015

# FOREWORD BY THE RIGHT REVEREND GRAHAM JAMES, BISHOP OF NORWICH

Anna Hinderer (then Anna Martin) was just twelve years old when she asked if she could care for some younger children at Sunday School. That was in 1839 at St Margaret's, Lowestoft. She was fortunate that the rector's wife at the time came from a Quaker background and was not perturbed about giving young girls responsibility. Early Victorian England could be rather more radical than we imagine. Nowadays it is doubtful that such a ready response would be made to a child at that age. Anna was given care of six younger children. Within a year or two she had proved herself such a good teacher and leader that she was given charge of a class of two hundred.

All this we learn from Ann Meakin's book recounting the remarkable story of Anna Hinderer. Anna's own capacity to write letters and keep accounts of her experiences means she left us much rich source material. It is a remarkable story. Anna died at just 43, rests in a Norfolk churchyard and is commemorated as a 'noble woman' in the Lady Chapel of Liverpool Cathedral.

As I read of Anna's later life I became increasingly convinced the key moment was when that kindly adult said yes to her youthful aspiration to care for other children and teach them the Christian gospel. Later, after meeting and marrying her husband David, Anna would do just this for the rest of her life in the Yoruba territory of West Africa under the auspices of the Church Missionary Society.

Theirs was no easy mission, partly because of civil war and the limited contact with other CMS mission stations.

What makes this story particularly worth telling is that it isn't one of immediate and resounding success. David and Anna based their mission on friendship and faithful propagation of the gospel.

They sought to establish good relationships with their neighbours including those who continued to be devoted to native African religions. The violence of so many local traditions presented the greatest challenge. Many of those who responded to the gospel faced ill treatment within their families and kinship groups. Anna and her husband also suffered incapacitating fevers. You wonder at their constancy and endurance.

While David was the preacher and innovator, often away searching out new areas for further mission stations, it was Anna who presided over the mission compound. It was both their family home and a refuge for children and young people, some abandoned, others seeking faith and a few whose lives had been transformed by the gospel. It was no accident that the next generation of Anglican Christian leadership in that part of Nigeria was formed and shaped by those who had been in Anna's care. She had her disappointments. These are faithfully recorded. She did not live to see the full fruits of her labours but few people in Christian ministry are given that blessing. As St Ignatius Loyola put it in his prayer, we are asked to *"toil and not to seek for rest; to labour and not to ask for any reward, save that of knowing that we do your will."*

Anna Hinderer did God's will. This is her story – a daughter of Norfolk for whom, thanks to Ann Meakin, the Diocese of Norwich and its people are now enabled to offer fresh and informed prayers of thanksgiving.

# ILLUSTRATIONS

# PREFACE

Anna's story was first publicised in a Memorial Book entitled 'Seventeen years in the Yoruba country'. The book was lovingly compiled by the daughters of the Revd. Richard Hone - Rector of Halesowen - who were close friends and great admirers. Following Anna's death they collected as many of her letters as could be obtained and, together with the information from her journal and other sources, produced the book. It sold very well, but it appears to be unobtainable now and is out of copyright. One copy survives in the Robarts Library at the University of Toronto, Canada and can now be read online. This biography includes information which has been discovered during recent research but also uses numerous quotations of Anna's words from the previous book. They describe her world more eloquently than anyone else could even though the language may seem somewhat archaic to twenty first century readers.

My first acquaintance with Anna was many decades ago when I chanced on a newspaper cutting, stored in the 'Local Studies' section at the old Norwich Central Library and read that the girls and staff of Kudeti High School (at Ibadan in Nigeria) had raised money for the repair of her grave in the churchyard at Martham where I live. My interest was kindled but it was many years before I realised that I could discover more about Anna via the internet. As my research progressed, such a moving story emerged that I felt that it deserved to be retold to people of the 21st century. I discovered that in the mid 19$^{th}$ century Anna and her husband David were very well known in Christian circles for their amazing pioneering missionary work in the Yoruba country of West Africa. How was it that they came to Martham where Anna found great joy and peace? What led Anna and David to the mission field in the first place? I became more and more fascinated and amazed at their bravery as their incredible story unfolded.

# INTRODUCTION

Few Norfolk girls have shown such commitment, courage and determination in the face of adversity that they have been considered worthy to be commemorated in a stained glass window in one of England's great cathedrals. Anna Hinderer, however, was an exceptional person.

When the windows for the Lady Chapel of the magnificent modern gothic Cathedral in the bustling port city of Liverpool were being designed in 1909, it was decided that they should depict 21 'Noble Women' of particular virtue who had made a significant contribution to helping the world. A condition was that they must be no longer living, preferably have a connection with Liverpool and be particularly admired at that time when the Cathedral was nearing completion. Surprisingly, few of the 'Noble Women' are remembered today.

One of the 'Noble Women' was Anna Hinderer, a pioneer missionary who died in 1870. Her grave is far away on the eastern side of England in the shadow of the chancel of the equally magnificent cathedral-like mediaeval Parish Church in the quiet village of Martham in windswept East Norfolk. Anna was the treasured, gentle and courageous wife of the Reverend David Hinderer, the assistant curate at Martham, who, many years later, was laid to rest with her.

# Chapter 1 Anna's Early Life

Anna was born at Hempnall in Norfolk on the 19th March 1827, the daughter of William and Margaret Martin. Her baptism is not recorded in the Parish Register there, but surprisingly it has been found in the Register at Wattisfield Independent Chapel over the border in Suffolk as is that of her younger brother William Woodroffe who was born at Long Stratton in 1830. Very little is known of Anna's early life. Sadly her mother, a very devout Christian, died in 1832 when Anna was just five years old, yet had already been a great influence on her daughter. In a letter of 1868 Anna wrote: 'I lost my dear mother when I was just five years old. I have just the remembrance of a form in bed, as white as a lily, with rather large bright blue eyes; and I know she taught me to sew; and when I was not by her bed-side, I used to sit on a low broad window-seat, and when I had done ten stitches, I was rewarded with a strawberry; and I used to say little tiny texts to her in the morning. I was only allowed to be in her room twice a day. But though I knew so little of her on earth, if God who is rich in mercy will have mercy on me, and admit me to His blest abode, I shall see her again, for she rejoiced in her God and Saviour, and I have been told that her last breath was spent in singing a few lines of a favourite hymn'.

So Anna and her younger brother grew up with their father who married again a year after Margaret had died and then five more children were born into the family. Her father was a merchant grocer and the family moved several times. The youngest children were born at Aylsham, Norfolk.

Did Anna go to school? That is not known but Anna certainly had a sound basic education and a good command of written English as her journal and letters reveal. Also like all girls of her generation she became proficient in needlework which she had started to learn at a very young age. In 1839, when Anna was 12 years old, her grandfather, John Martin, who had a harness-making business in Lowestoft High Street, and her Aunt Mary who kept house for him, invited her to stay with them. Harness-making was an important trade in Lowestoft in those days, when the more wealthy townspeople went about in their horse-drawn carriages and the farmers of the surrounding countryside used horses for heavy farm work and to pull their carts and wagons. Anna was of an age when many girls would have gone into domestic service or found other work, so it was not surprising that she should leave home at that time. The family were probably living at Lowestoft then, so thinking that the sea air at Lowestoft would continue to be beneficial to her health, her father agreed that she should go to stay with her grandfather. To him, she would have been a useful addition to the household and business. This was the beginning of the chain of astonishing events that formed her life. Anna later wrote that 'the providential leading guiding hand' stretched out for her future good.

Lowestoft High Street. The gap to the left of the houses is the site of John Martin's harness-making business where Anna lived during her teenage years.

While she was living with her grandfather, Anna went with him to St. Margaret's Church – the ancient medieval Parish

Church of Lowestoft. She loved the beauty and solemnity of the services there. Anna later wrote: 'I loved Sunday above every day. I loved church, and was soon permitted to enter into the beauty and solemnity of the services. I felt I was in a holy place, and that holy words were being used. The whole service was frequently read through by me in the week, and I found fresh beauties in it, which I could comprehend. I felt there was something magnificent in it, and my mind would feed upon it, and soar away in imagination from many of its passages. The Te Deum [a canticle sung at the service of Matins] carried me to heaven. I longed to be a martyr, to be one of that noble army. 'Vouchsafe, O Lord, to keep me this day without sin,' became a daily prayer; yet I did not entirely call upon Him who only can take away sin, the precious and only Saviour. 'Almighty God, unto whom all hearts be open and from whom no secrets are hid,' made me afraid of sin, and when inclined to do wrong, and be naughty, that passage would come into my mind, so that I feared; but it was not the fear of grieving my God and Saviour. However, I was graciously and gradually led on step by step. I cannot tell of times and seasons, but I became more and more happy. I longed to do something. I had a strong desire to become a missionary, to give myself up to some holy work, and had a firm belief that such a calling would be mine. I think this came from a wish to be a martyr ....'

(Lowestoft has altered greatly since Anna's days there. At that time, the magnificent medieval Parish Church of St. Margaret stood over half a mile inland from the sea on elevated ground in splendid isolation in the open countryside. The sight of that church with its slender spire topped with a gilded weathercock soaring skywards must have been a spectacular one from a vast distance across the surrounding fields and from the sea. It is now surrounded by twentieth century housing estates.

For many centuries Lowestoft people had been employed in the fishing industry, so as new land was forming on the beach below the cliffs, people were building homes there and the town was growing seawards. Because of the distance to the Parish Church, in 1833 St. Peter's Church – a daughter church of St.

Margaret's - was opened to serve the people who lived along the High Street and in the expanding part of the town nearer to the sea and the new harbour.

Lowestoft suffered major damage from bombing during the 1939 to 1945 war, necessitating the building of many new homes. In the 1970s increasing road traffic meant that a major new road system was required. Sadly, St. Peter's Church had to be demolished in 1975 to accommodate the new lay-out of that part of the town.)

St. Margaret's Church, Lowestoft
(Photograph by Seajay Harrison)

During Anna's time in Lowestoft the Vicar was the Reverend Francis Cunningham. His wife, Richenda, was also very much involved in the ministry in the parish and was in charge of the Sunday school. The Cunninghams lived in a fine Vicarage on Lowestoft cliff top with a beautiful 'hanging' garden at the back, created to cling to the cliff face with steps leading down to the beach. (The house was demolished as a result of bomb damage during the war of 1939 to 1945 and the site is now a green space with trees. The garden is now part of the wildlife friendly wilderness on the cliff face.) Francis and Richenda Cunningham kept 'open house' for all, as had been a tradition in the family in Norwich in which Mrs Cunningham grew up. Parishioners came and went as they pleased and friends and relatives from further away were frequent visitors.

Anna later described how she came to know Mr. and Mrs. Cunningham. 'Dear Mr. and Mrs. Cunningham knew little of me then; they looked kindly at me often, as they did at everyone, and he used often to ask me my name. I often thought if I might have a few little children in the Sunday-school to teach, it would be an immense pleasure. I was afraid to ask it, but having obtained my aunt's consent, when I was between twelve and thirteen, I ventured one Saturday, after passing dear Mrs. Cunningham three times, to make my request, fearing all the time that she would say I was too young and too small; but what was my joy when she smiled so kindly upon me (I shall never forget that smile, I have the most vivid remembrance of it), and told me to go to the school at eight o'clock the next morning, and she would give me a class. I was up early enough; a heavy snow was upon the ground, but that was nothing. I went, and six little ones were committed to my care; and thus commenced that intensely interesting work, to which, I may say, I more and more entirely devoted myself to the last Sunday of my time in that place.

My introduction to the Sunday-school led to an introduction into the Vicarage. Dearest Mrs. Cunningham, with her natural kindness, wished me to go to tea on Sunday evenings sometimes; this grew into a regular custom, and one evening she asked me to go and sit with her while she was drawing; I read to her, and then left. She then wished me to go every morning at ten o'clock, and see how things stood;

The Reverend Francis Cunningham

Richenda Cunningham

and sometimes I remained there, at others I went away. I became very much occupied. Dear Mr. Cunningham employed me too. I copied for him, and became a district visitor. The more I had to do, the happier I was. My life was given for them; the very atmosphere was just the thing for me, and each day I only loved them more and more. In time I resided altogether under their roof. Oh, they were happy years. I found my way amongst the people; my love for the school-children found an entrance for me to the mothers' hearts, and I had many friends among high and low, rich and poor.'

As Anna lived at her grandfather's home and workshop in the High Street just a few hundred yards away from the Vicarage, it was very convenient for Anna to visit there. The Cunninghams had very soon become aware that she was bright and enthusiastic and always willing to be helpful. The Reverend Francis Cunningham, finding that she could do useful clerical and secretarial work for him, even asked her to write some of the entries in the Parish Registers as her hand writing was beautifully legible. As time went by, Mr. Cunningham took her with him when he went to call on parishioners. Soon Anna was allocated her own area of Lowestoft for which she was responsible for visiting and in addition was even appointed to teach the boys at The Workhouse.

(This meant a walk of two and a half miles in each direction as the Mutford and Lothingland Workhouse built to care for the paupers and orphaned children of Lowestoft and the neighbouring villages, was in the village of Oulton. The Workhouse has been demolished and replaced with modern housing. All that remains is the little pauper's cemetery without a single grave stone recording who is buried there.)

Anna was such a gifted teacher that before long she was presiding over a Sunday school of over 200 children for an hour every Sunday. It seems likely that Anna may also have taught at the schools across the road from the Vicarage where a petrol station now stands. Those schools were under the management of the clergy and churchwardens.)

Maybe it was because Anna had become indispensable in the household, that eventually the Cunninghams invited her to live with them. They had no children of their own, so perhaps Anna was the daughter they had hoped for. Francis and Richenda Cunningham were remarkable people. Fortunately they had seen Anna's potential and, perhaps unwittingly, gave her the best training and preparation she could possibly have received for her future life.

Francis Cunningham was a clergyman of the Evangelical tradition. He was Rector of Pakefield from 1814 until 1830 when he became Vicar of Lowestoft. He died at Lowestoft in 1863 at the age of 78 having enjoyed just three years of retirement.

But what of Richenda's background? Richenda's early life was spent in Gurney Court in Norwich. She was the sixth of the twelve children of John and Catherine Gurney who were staunch members of the Quaker Meeting (The Society of Friends) at Norwich. A few years later, in greater prosperity, the family moved to a very grand home at Earlham Hall on the western outskirts of Norwich. There, Richenda grew up and that amazing Quaker family welcomed to their home many of the most famous and influential people of the day.

Her older sister, always called Betsy by the family, married Joseph Fry, became the famous prison reformer Elizabeth Fry and is another of the 21 'Noble Women' commemorated in Liverpool Cathedral. Her sister Hannah married Sir Thomas Fowell Buxton - known as 'The Liberator' - who was a leading campaigner against slavery and is now commemorated with a memorial plaque on the wall of the Bauchon Chapel in Norwich Cathedral. One brother was Samuel Gurney, the banker who became one of the richest men in the world, a great philanthropist to the people of the East End of London and a generous benefactor to charitable causes.

Among her achievements, Richenda was a very skilled artist, having had lessons from the most talented painter in Norwich at that time, John Crome, (a member of the Norwich school of painters) known affectionately as 'Old Crome'. Anna certainly learned a great deal from Richenda and became very accomplished in drawing, leaving a wonderful legacy of sketches of scenes from her later life.

The Cunninghams were great travellers and went on tours throughout the UK and Europe. It seems that sometimes they left Anna to run the household which she must have done very efficiently. On the 1851 census form she was listed as the 'housekeeper' at the house adjoining the 'Vicarage House'. By this time Anna, with her sparkling personality and all the capabilities and attributes she had acquired, would have appeared to be a most suitable wife for any intelligent middle class man. Was marriage to be her destiny? All her life Anna had longed to become a missionary.

Later in her life when she looked back at this time she wrote: 'Notwithstanding all, my old desire for a missionary life would never leave me, and, though so much of my work at home was of a missionary character, yet I felt that to heathen lands I was to go, and that such would be my calling some day, though I never saw the least shadow as to how it was to be accomplished. Yet often so near did it seem to be, that I suffered much in the thought of the cost it would be to give up all that I so tenderly loved. And in school, on a hot summer's day, when weary and dispirited, I would be roused and refreshed by the thought of the contrast between my present position and that of the missionary in other lands, under a burning sun, and other trials; and then the thought of how soon I might be called to one of those lands, and have to give up those dear children, then entrusted to my care, would bring a tear to my eye, and give me a fresh stimulus to make use of my present opportunities with them; and that text Jeremiah xii. 5 has given me fresh vigour and power. Yet, although all this time no way in the smallest degree seemed to open for such a thing, He who only knoweth the future steps of His children was preparing me in a way I understood not.' (In the Authorized Version of the Bible, Jeremiah xii. 5 says "how wilt thou do in the swelling of Jordan?")

Then, quite suddenly, Anna's future was revealed to her. The Reverend David Hinderer, a priest who had been working for the Church Missionary Society (CMS) in West Africa, came into her life. In a very short time she knew exactly where she would be going. After what must have been a whirlwind romance, Anna in great joy told a friend 'It's all settled; I am going to be married to Mr. Hinderer, and we are going to Ibadan.' The friend tells how 'Having made the decision that she was to be a missionary's wife, she fearlessly and trustfully went forth. I remember that time so well. She was wonderfully happy and bright in the prospect. She did not seem to see the difficulties before her. Her eye rested on the work and its reward, and her courage never failed.'

Anna and David were married at St. Margaret's Church, the magnificent ancient mediaeval Parish Church of Lowestoft, on 14th October 1852 by which time Anna was 24 and David was 32. The wedding was in the presence of Anna's family and friends and a host of the Cunninghams' friends and relatives. A friend who was present at the marriage wrote that, 'The fine old church was thronged from end to end; the school-children, lining the path to the churchyard gate, scattered flowers before the bride and bridegroom. These are common-place incidents - everybody was there; it was regarded almost as a public festival'. Anna and David made their vows to each other, promising to be husband and wife 'for better, for worse, for richer, for poorer, in sickness, and in health…' little realising the poignancy of these promises for them. It truly seemed to be a marriage made in heaven.

The same friend continued, 'The wedding breakfast was by no means common-place. Among the speeches was one from Mrs. Cunningham herself. To her, with her hereditary connection with the Society of Friends, it was the most natural thing in the world to do; and well do I remember the breathless silence with which her affectionate and impressive words were listened to.' (In those days it was very unusual for a woman to speak in public as it was not considered to be 'lady-like' to do so. However, the members of the Society of Friends were much more enlightened and encouraged everyone to develop and use their talents to the full.)

THE REV. DAVID HINDERER,
*C.M.S. Missionary in the Yoruba Country, 1849—1877.*

Among the many wedding presents was a bound book of blank pages to be Anna's journal. This gift was from the very perceptive and far sighted Francis Cunningham and was to prove invaluable. At the beginning of the book he wrote: 'Given to

Anna Martin, by the Rev. Francis Cunningham, the friend of her youth, and the minister to her in maturer years, until she was called to devote herself to the blessed service of missions in Africa.' It is from its pages that we have first-hand knowledge of Anna's adventurous life after her marriage. Anna fervently looked forward to accompanying David when he returned to Africa. She wrote later that 'she rejoiced in the thought of living and dying for Africa' because she had for such a long time felt a calling to become a missionary.

What was David's background? It is slightly puzzling to look through the alumni of students of Oxford and Cambridge universities and not find him. Those were the days when almost all clergy were 'Oxbridge' educated. As he had been working for the Church Missionary Society their records were explored. The Church Missionary Society (CMS) was originally set up to campaign against slavery, the mission to evangelise coming later. Included among those who set up the organisation was William Wilberforce who had been a guest of the Gurneys at Earlham Hall. After slavery was officially abolished throughout almost all of the British Empire in 1834, evangelism became an increasing possibility. Termination of the European slave trade not only opened opportunities for the development of other trade but also for Christian missionaries to preach their message.

The CMS expected that there would be numerous members of the clergy from the Anglican Church who would be applying to go abroad as missionaries. That did not happen. Therefore the CMS had to look further afield to Europe to find young men who were willing and keen to respond to the call to take up that work. The greatest response came from men of the Lutheran Church. Among these was the young David Hinderer from the seminary at Basle.

David – a farmer's son - had been born in 1819 at Weisbuch near Schorndorf in Wurtemberg, now part of Germany. As a young man he had learned to be a highly skilled craftsman. However, feeling the call to Christian ministry, he went for training to the seminary at Basle and was there when he heard of the need for missionaries. He came to England in 1846 for further training in London at the CMS College at Islington, was ordained a priest in the Church of England in 1848 by Bishop Blomfield and went to the Yoruba country of West Africa in 1849. His linguistic skills must have been incredibly good as English was not his first language and he seems have become fluent in Yoruba very quickly.

European missionaries first ventured into the interior of West Africa in the 1840s after the slave trade had officially ended – although slaving remained a heavily engaged activity amongst warring local tribes. Intrepid travellers first arrived by ship at Lagos, the port where those visiting that part of West Africa disembarked. From there it was possible to venture inland northwards by river boats and cross-country tracks. One of the large towns inland was Abeokuta and it was there that the Church Missionary Society opened a mission station in 1845. It was while serving with the CMS team there that David heard that a caravan of traders was going to Ibadan about 50 miles further to the north east. The traders allowed him to join them.

In 1851 David was thought to be the first white man to go to Ibadan. He was certainly the first European missionary. The townspeople were absolutely amazed to see this 'oyinbo' (white man) and the town's chiefs gave him a very warm welcome. He stayed there for five months before returning to Abeokuta.

Ibadan, in the kingdom of Oyo, was by that time a sprawling and rapidly developing 'new' town surrounded by seven hills. It had a very complex history which is far beyond the scope of this book. For centuries it had been at the junction of trade routes which crossed the African continent. Therefore, it was not surprising that people began to settle there.

During the 1820s Yoruba people fleeing from tribal conflicts and persecutions elsewhere arrived at Ibadan in huge numbers. Town walls were built for everyone's protection. They enclosed an area about six miles across within which there were compounds of single storey buildings surrounding a square or rectangular courtyard. Most of the compounds were surrounded by a plot of land where the inhabitants could grow much of their food. But there were also vacant plots of land.

JOURNEY OF THE REV. D. HINDERER TO IBADAN.

Ibadan was governed by a group of chiefs who exercised strict control. In most instances people did not pay rent but the chiefs allocated land at their discretion for new buildings. With such a diversity of people from numerous tribes, speaking their own dialects and bringing with them their religious practices, customs and traditions, not surprisingly Ibadan was a place of turbulence. It had become a major centre for trade and commerce and also still for the slave trade among the local tribes.

Fulani Muslims from the northeast were already well settled in the town and their influence was continually increasing. Coming from the area of Lake Chad, they had already conquered all of the country of the Hausa people who lived in the area which is now the northern part of the present country of Nigeria. It was because of the Fulani Muslim presence that David felt that there was an urgent need for preaching the Christian gospel there. Certainly it presented a great challenge. Indeed, he duly realised that this was not work he could do alone. He needed assistance. This necessitated his return to England to seek help from the CMS, which proved to be a timely return as it was also deemed advisable for the sake of his health.

In those days when missionaries returned home on furlough they were in great demand as speakers to church congregations who were interested in their work. Also of course it was important to go to inform people of their activities in order to persuade them to give generously to the Society's funds. For David, his visit to Lowestoft proved more exceptionally rewarding than he had anticipated.

For Anna and David the first challenge in their married life came very soon. It was to gather together and pack everything needed to set up a home and establish a mission at Ibadan.

Anna and David Hinderer

## Chapter 2 The beginning of the journey

Organising the transport of all their household goods and equipment for Africa must have been logistically very demanding for Anna and David. They had less than two months in which to do it. All their clothes and household soft furnishings had to be packed into wooden chests lined with lead. (A lead lining may have seemed an expensive inclusion but it was very important as they discovered many years later.)

Not long before leaving for Africa, Anna saw a document at the CMS Office which bothered her slightly. It was a list of the Church Missionary Society's missionaries and their length of service. Against those who had served in West Africa she read 'one year', 'five months', 'six weeks' .....! She apparently said to David, 'I do trust that God will give us a little longer than that to live and work for Him. Don't you hope so?' David is said to have replied with a story as follows: 'I will tell you how it is. It was large and strong and fenced up to heaven. An army encompassed that city to besiege it and take it. For long years they fought, but still they took it not. It was destined that they should conquer and they knew it. But yet, long time passed; whole ranks of the army fell; and that city stood yet untaken. Now this was the reason wherefore they could not prevail against it. Round about the city was a very large trench. So deep and wide was it that because thereof the army could not approach near enough to throw down the walls. Still they would not raise the siege, until at last they found that that mighty trench had been quite filled up with the dead bodies of their fellow soldiers, who had fallen in the fight. Then they marched over them and they took the city.'

'Now so it is with Africa. Long time our brethren have been attacking the strongholds of Satan there, though as yet they have not stormed it. But we who come after will conquer by the grace of God. Look (and he pointed once more to the names), those are only the bodies of our soldiers filling up the trench. We will not fear them. We will step over them boldly in the name of our God and we will take the city, will we not?' It is said that 'Yes dear, we will', was Anna's ardent reply.

Anna and David then travelled to Plymouth, presumably by train as by then the railways had covered every region of England. From there, on 6$^{th}$ December 1852, after waiting several days for suitable weather, they sailed on the mail steamer ship Propontis which at that time was making regular trips from England to Capetown, a trip scheduled to last 40 days and calling at numerous African ports en route. The *Propontis* was one of a new fleet of most prestigious ships of the General Screw Steam Shipping Company built to serve the increasing demand for journeys between England and the expanding colonies, carrying mail (some of it containing very valuable items), cargo and a few passengers.

The S.S. Propontis (from the collection of C. John Cotton)

Several of the other missionaries who embarked with them were mentioned by Anna. Those included were Bishop Owen Emeric Vidal who was the first Bishop of Sierra Leone, Mrs. Vidal, the Reverend Richard and Mrs. Paley, Mr. Hensman who was to be a medical missionary, Mr. Kefer who was to work alongside David at Ibadan, Mr. Gerst and Mr. Maser. (People were not on

Christian name terms except with close friends and family in those days.) It was a terrible voyage. The Bay of Biscay was so rough that Anna stayed in her cabin for the first four days hardly able even to rise from her bunk. She was utterly seasick and homesick but recovered enough to enjoy going ashore at Madeira. On 23rd December they reached the port at Bathurst, Gambia. Anna and David sat out on the deck on a peaceful calm evening and watched a beautiful sunset. They also went ashore for Anna to touch African soil for the first time. By 27$^{th}$ December they were in the port of Freetown, Sierra Leone, where they bade farewell to Bishop and Mrs Vidal who disembarked to a rapturous welcome from a huge crowd waiting on the quay.

(It was of particular importance for Sierra Leone which was a British Colony to have a resident Bishop for pastoral care of the local clergy. There were also several African men in training for the priesthood but as only a bishop was allowed to hold a service of ordination, they would all have had to travel to England to be ordained. There were also many African Christians who had been baptised and looked forward to being confirmed by a bishop).

Eventually on 5$^{th}$ January 1853, the *Propontis*, carrying Anna and David, anchored off Lagos. In those days before the harbour had been built, all passengers and cargo had to be transferred to smaller boats as because seagoing ships could not cross the sand bar to enter the lagoon. (The new harbour was several decades in the future.) Lagos was a rapidly developing town, sprawling across low-lying swampy islands between the lagoon and the sea and on to the mainland. It was a haven for runaway slaves. Freed slaves returning from the Americas were also welcomed as many had become highly skilled craftsmen. At one time Lagos had been a Portuguese trading post, later it became a major slave trading port. However, by 1852 the British Navy had taken control in order to try to put an end to the slave trade. The CMS then decided that the Mission that had been established at Badagry should be transferred there.

Anna and David planned to stay there briefly with the missionaries, the Reverend and Mrs. Gollmer, so that they could acclimatise to Africa. Ironically they received the first letters from home (which had actually sailed with them) including one from the Cunninghams which Anna was delighted to receive. On 13th January 1853 when they were almost ready to depart towards their destination at Ibadan, Anna fell ill with her first bout of fever. This was the dreaded yellow fever which affected all Europeans before preventative vaccination. It was a viral infection caused by being bitten by one of the infected mosquitoes which, in the Lagos area, bred freely in the swampy land between the Lagos Lagoon and the sea. Quinine was the only medicine available at that time to alleviate the symptoms and lower the temperature. It was because of devastating tropical diseases like yellow fever that Africa became known as 'the white man's grave'. Large numbers of the early travellers and missionaries died very swiftly after falling ill.

After being on her bed for a week, and a further few days getting her strength back, on 26th January 1853 Anna felt fit enough to face the journey northwards.

For financial support David was paid a quarterly allowance while serving with the Church Missionary Society. Before travelling inland from Lagos he needed to exchange the dollars he had been given for the local currency – the cumbersome cowrie shells - so that they could buy the necessities they had not brought with them and pay for other services. Cowries came in strings of 40 or 100 or 20,000 to a sack full. It was not exactly a convenient currency to handle or carry about. David and Anna would need to pay the people who would be working for them at the Mission and everyone would need food too. Establishing the Mission would be a costly project requiring careful financial management.

For the journey to Abeokuta, Anna and David travelled with a huge escort party of men to carry their goods, chattels and possessions and to protect them from unwelcome wildlife. Anna wrote: 'We left Lagos on the 26th of January, and went up the

River Ogun in canoes. There was much to enjoy; the scenery was magnificent; such banks, foliage, flowers, scented shrubs, exquisite little birds red, purple, orange, yellow, green besides plenty of chattering monkeys and parrots. The nights were the time of trial, yet we had the moon, and a most brilliant one it was, to cheer us. The first night we had to stop at a little town, and were allowed to pitch our tents in a small market-place. Our men made a fire on the ground, and boiled some water, and we had tea, which refreshed us greatly. Hundreds of people sat round to look at us, and clapped their hands and shouted to see us eat. They were kind enough to retire about eleven, and, though surrounded by goats, fowls, and dogs, I slept soundly in our tent, on a mattress on the ground.

We were off by six the next morning, with all the people to watch our departure. The morning air was delicious, the water-lilies most fragrant and lovely. The next two nights we pitched our tents on sand-banks close by the river, and had several large fires to keep off the wild animals; nevertheless, a baboon and some foxes had a great desire to make our acquaintance, but a man fired a gun and sent them flying. Still there were many things that made a queer noise all night. The insects were my worst enemies; I could not close my eyes, so I sat at the opening of the tent, watching the moon, and our black men sleeping close to the fires. We left at two o' clock on the third morning, the moon gave us the opportunity of leaving at this early hour and we parted with our canoes at a place called Agbamaya, in the middle of the day, where Mr. Crowther, his son, and several people were kind enough to come and meet us.'

This meeting with the Reverend Samuel Ajayi Crowther was a wonderfully welcoming and auspicious one. Had he been waiting several days anxiously wondering why their canoes had not appeared? David would have known him well from his previous stay in Abeokuta. Samuel Crowther was a Yoruba native who as a boy had been brutally snatched by slave traders with a great many people from his home town but freed when their slave ship was intercepted by the British Navy. He was put ashore at Sierra

Leone where he was educated at a Christian school, baptised with an English name, sent to England for further education and became the first Yoruba native priest. On a visit to England he was a guest of Sir Thomas Fowell Buxton and his wife Hannah at Northrepps, Norfolk and preached in Northrepps Church in 1843. He translated the New Testament and The Book of Common Prayer into Yoruba. In 1853 he was part of the team at the Abeokuta Mission having been a co-founder with the Revd. Henry Townsend.

Abeokuta was a very large market town on a rocky outcrop on the east bank of the River Ogun with 18 miles of mud walls surrounding it for protection. The Yoruba people in the town were of the Egba tribe who had settled there about 1825 as refugees fleeing from slave hunters. Over one hundred towns and villages had been abandoned in terror of the kidnappers and slave traders. The Church Missionary Society founded the Mission there in 1845.

GATEWAY OF AN AFRICAN TOWN.

Anna continued, 'The Chief of Oshielle sent a horse for my husband; I was put in a hammock, and did not wake till put down on the ground outside the town wall. I could hardly believe that I really opened my eyes upon Abeokuta. The past has seemed so much like a dream. We had still to go two miles further to a house vacated by missionaries now in England, not very inviting in its appearance. The white ants had eaten holes in the floor and walls, and insects of various kinds haunted it, spiders as large as the palm of your hand, and many others. We arrived in the last rays of daylight. My husband began to unpack the stores and things he could put his hand upon; our good boy Olubi helped him and the cook killed a fowl, and boiled eggs, which happily were to be had close by our gate. I had to get out sheets for our bed. Then we sat down to tea, laughing heartily at our first attempt at housekeeping. We went early to rest, tired enough, and I slept till the ringing of a bell awoke me a little before six, to usher in the blessed Sabbath morning, and to call the people to prayer, which they conduct among themselves. The school met at nine: a most interesting sight, young and old assembled together, and as earnest as possible over their books. I thought of my own dear children at home, and tears flowed abundantly. I went to both the services, and though I could hardly understand one word, yet I greatly enjoyed it, and felt that I was in God's house, and that He was there.'

The boy Olubi mentioned above was known to David from his earlier time in Abeokuta. He was an intelligent young man who became their first true African friend. Anna told that his mother was a priestess of the god Igun and as a baby he had been dedicated to the god Abatala. Like many Africans he had been angry to hear the white men's open air preaching but following an accident, he was unable to walk away when one of the other missionaries started to speak and so could not avoid hearing what he said. He listened and thought, 'It is not anything bad he is saying.' He was curious about the white man's worship, so went to a service and thought it was wonderfully inspiring. Much to his mother's dismay, he wanted to continue attending and was baptised and given the name Daniel. When he agreed to go to Ibadan with David and Anna a deep and long-lasting friendship developed.

The Yoruba people responded instantly to Anna's very warm personality even though she could not as yet speak to them in their own Yoruba language. They sang English hymns to her which made her feel very tearful. By 18th February Anna was severely ill again with fever and unable to get up from her mattress for several days. However she was much cheered by the arrival on 23rd February of the harmonium which Richenda Cunningham had bought for them. Anna of course could play it but one of the local chiefs when invited to have a go, could not get a sound from it. Had he not noticed the action of Anna's feet on the pedals pumping the air for the bellows? From that time onwards the harmonium accompanied the Saturday evening hymn singing which was as great a feature of the mission as it had been at Lowestoft Vicarage in Anna's youth.

Once Anna had recovered from the fever, David left on 3rd March for Ibadan to visit the chiefs and to receive permission for them to set up home there. This involved another dangerous 50 mile overland trek on narrow paths through the bush. It was the first time he and Anna had been separated since their marriage and she admitted to feeling very miserable and apprehensive about it. While he was away, Anna continued to learn Yoruba and made good friends with the local children. She played ball with them early in the morning when it was not too hot and was happy to report that she felt fully fit again.

The other missionaries were not so fortunate. Mr. and Mrs. Paley, Mr. Maser and Mr. Hensman with whom they had sailed to Africa were all extremely ill with fever and in spite of Anna's careful nursing Mr. Paley died. When Mrs. Paley recovered she decided to return to England but, sadly, died on the voyage. Mr. Hensman the medical missionary also died but not from yellow fever. On the 4th Sunday after Easter, Anna read the collect and was greatly comforted. 'O Almighty God, who alone canst order the unruly wills and affections of sinful men: Grant unto thy people, that they may love the thing which thou commandest, and desire that which thou dost promise: that so, among the sundry and manifold changes of the world, our hearts may surely there be fixed, where true joys are to be found; through Jesus Christ our Lord. Amen.'

On David's return from Ibadan they both prepared for their journey there and on 25th April set off on the next stage of their journey – the 50 mile trek across the beautiful and constantly changing countryside that Anna greatly enjoyed.

## Chapter 3 Arrival at Ibadan and settling into the first home there

Leaving Abeokuta, Anna and David started their journey on horseback, accompanied on foot by the servants they had recruited and a great company of men to protect them and to carry their enormous collection of goods and chattels. The journey is best described in Anna's words: 'We journeyed on and on, one behind the other, very quietly, with our long train of attendant carriers, full of thought of the past and future. There was something to admire around, good pasture and beautiful cattle. Our silence was broken, and we talked of the goodness and mercy which had so surrounded our path in the midst of our sorrow and trials, during our short sojourn in Abeokuta, and we could look forward with confiding hope and trust, and take comfort and courage in that we were following the leading of a gracious Providence. And now we were on our way to this long-talked-of town, to attack, in the name of the Lord of Hosts, this stronghold of sin and Satan.

I tried in the stillness of the bush to draw near to the Living Fountain, to seek help, comfort, and protection in our great undertaking, and I had some precious hours. I soon left my little horse to Olubi's care, and got into my hammock, for I was tired. I certainly may say that I have had no little to do the last month or six weeks, so that I did enjoy the rest of this hammock, with its cradle-like motion; and a little refreshing breeze sprang up. We did not reach our resting-place till quite dusk, but the tent was quickly up, and we had bright lanterns, comfortable tea, and prayers, and our people were soon fast asleep on their mats. We walked about by moonlight, we were within reach of the dwellings of man, and people were passing backwards and forwards from and to their farms, the greater part of the night.

We slept some hours, and after a nice breakfast in gypsy-like style, the next morning we pursued our journey. After an hour, we were quite in the bush. I did enjoy that day's journey; such nice cool air, trees and scented bushes twining together so thickly that even the African sun could not penetrate. Now and then we stopped to refresh ourselves and to change my carriers, and then sometimes we sang and sometimes talked. Many, many times we wished our dear good friends could take a peep at us.

We halted for the night, about five o'clock, on a rock which seems spread out on purpose for weary travellers, but alas there was no water. We had some in a bottle for our tea, but our poor attendants got none. However, with their usual easy nature, they each spread a mat on the hard rock; down they threw their weary bodies and in less than five minutes were fast asleep, except those who kept up the fires. I could not sleep. The whole scene and circumstances were so novel. About eight o'clock the moon again rose majestically and a wonderful sight it was. We were now in the midst of the African bush, no human dwelling near us, but how different to what it once was, when the kidnappers haunted almost every bush, and wild animals were near. Now all our people were sleeping away, with their guns by their side truly, but only in case any kind of animal should be troublesome.

I was very glad to see the morning light, to start quite early, and to sleep without any nervous apprehension in my hammock. When I awoke I found myself on another rock, with our fellow travellers watching my sweet repose; and they enjoyed a good laugh when I opened my eyes. In the middle of this rock was most delicious water, and very deep; it made us think of the provision God made for the children of Israel from a stony rock. Our people drank heartily, and we had a delicious cup of tea under a mangrove tree, and finding a nice little brook close by, we washed, and put on tidy clothes, that we might make a respectable appearance in Ibadan, which we expected to reach in a few hours.

I now mounted my horse, but certainly it was not so easy jumping over big trees. At the next halting-place we saw large tracts of land covered with Indian corn and cotton trees, and the immense town of Ibadan appearing at about two miles distance. It was a beautiful sight, and now my faithful affectionate men, for so

I must call them, nearly began to quarrel as to who should carry me into the town, for be carried in my hammock I must, according to their desire.'

In the same way that white people were very curious about black people, the black people were absolutely fascinated with David, the first white man they had ever seen. So, the anticipation of a white woman as well was bound to be a major excitement. Even though Anna and David wished to make a good impression on the people of Ibadan, they were perhaps totally unprepared for the very exuberant reception they received.

'We waited at the town wall, and heard that the chief was out of town at one of his farms, so we went in and through it, to our little dwelling, which is quite out of it at the other side. But as soon as we touched the town there was such a scene, men, women, and children shouting and screaming, "The white man is come! Oibo de!" and "the white mother is come!" and then their thousands of salutations, everybody opening eyes and mouth at me. All seemed pleased, but many frightened too when I spoke; they followed us to our own dwelling with the most curious shouts, noises, and exclamations.

All seemed perfectly bewildered; horses, sheep, goats, did not know where or which way to go, even the pigeons looked ready to exclaim, "What is happening?" The people were good and kind enough to let us enter our house by ourselves, but many, many of them stood round about till sunset, just to catch a glimpse of the wonderful white woman; and every time I appeared, down they went on the ground, rubbing their hands, and saying, "Alafia, Alafia, peace, peace." We could but let them enjoy the treat, though we were not sorry when daylight fading warned them to depart, for with all our comforts and alleviations we were tired enough. We soon unpacked things sufficient for present necessity, and a good night's rest was very refreshing.'

By this time one can sense that Anna was becoming used to being a curiosity and a celebrity and although enjoying it and accepting it with grace and serenity, was realizing it came at a considerable price.

## The First Home

The vacant compound on Kudeti Hill that David had arranged to be their first home was very primitive – just rooms round a courtyard and water from a nearby stream. The main room was long and narrow and they made partitions with curtains so that they had a bedroom and a living room. Another room was for Mr. Kefer, another for a kitchen/store, while the servants, many of whom initially were Christian converts who had come with them from Abeokuta, slept on their mats in the open central courtyard. There was just a mud floor, mud walls and a flimsily thatched roof – no doors or windows. The only entrance was through a gap in the wall where they hung a curtain. It was surrounded by a little garden which they could cultivate themselves. The roof thatch was full of insects of numerous sorts that created horribly eerie sounds in the quietness of the night. Other creatures ran round the floor. One of the worst early experiences was when one night David got up and nearly put his foot on a snake which was poisonous but fortunately he had frightened it and it speedily slithered away.

Very quickly, Anna's friendly personality attracted people to her. Women realising that she was unused to the heat would bring great palm leaves with which to fan her. The children were always surrounding her and chattering away and wanted to hold her hand. Initially Anna ran the household with the help of African servants while David and Mr. Kefer went about the town preaching. From the start they held services in Yoruba every Sunday in their courtyard.

On May 8$^{th}$ 1853, their second Sunday, Anna wrote: 'Another blessed Sabbath-day; people remarkably attentive. They heard of Jesus for the first time, and seem much struck with the message of salvation. The past week has been one of much occupation, putting things to rights, and receiving no end of visitors from morning till evening. It requires a little tact and patience to meet the whole thing. I have had some nice little presents of yams, fowls, and fruit. Oh, for wisdom and patience to deal rightly and wisely with these people; to be willing to amuse and give myself up cheerfully to little things, if by any means I may win some. My dear husband is well, always occupied, and much interested in everything around him. We do enjoy finding ourselves in Ibadan, and a work, a great, a holy work, commenced. O God, give Thy blessing.'

A YORUBA COMPOUND.

Soon they were able to erect a building to serve as both church and schoolroom with a roof of palm leaves and an earth floor on which everybody sat. At the Sunday morning services they sang hymns accompanied on the harmonium by Anna and in common with everyone else in the Anglican Church, they used the services from the Book of Common Prayer of 1662. (The Reverend Samuel Crowther had already translated them into Yoruba.) At first the people did not understand what they were doing but gradually became enlightened and came to watch and then to join in.

The Africans very quickly picked up hymn tunes. Probably the sung words were easier to remember than spoken ones but it is not clear whether these were in English or Yoruba. They had hymn books which were a gift from Lowestoft but of course, at first they could not read the words. Hanging on the wall above the harmonium were pictures of Francis and Richenda Cunningham who had given it. These were a constant reminder of the friends back home who had given Anna so much and who Anna knew would be supporting them faithfully in their thoughts and prayers. On Sunday afternoons they soon started a Sunday school for adults as well as children, because inquiring adults were very keen to learn about Christianity and discuss things in a way that would have been difficult during a service of worship.

On weekdays they started a Mission School for the children who were being taught, among other things, to say The Lord's Prayer and Ten Commandments in Yoruba. One of the local chiefs sent his children to the school, which they loved. As the school was only in the mornings from nine until twelve noon, in the late afternoons when it was cooler, Anna sometimes went for walks with the children. In this way they talked and learned each other's languages. She would tell them the English names for things and they told her the Yoruba names. Anna very soon realised that they were much better at remembering than she was.

A constant problem was that frequently both Anna and David were plagued with bouts of fever in spite of taking quinine which they hoped would prevent it. Either Anna or David would be ill and need nursing by the other day and night. Days of illness were very frightening and were days of awful apprehension. They were extremely grateful for the presence of Daniel Olubi who had swiftly become a highly valued member of the household. He took great care of Mr Kefer when he succumbed to fever.

The occasional wonderful highlight in their days was the arrival of mail from home, brought by a passing caravan of traders. This happened about every three months following the arrival of a ship from England. When, on 23rd May the first mail arrived in

Ibadan, Anna's excitement was very great. She wrote, 'You can hardly think what the sight even of a kind friend's handwriting is, in this far-off land. Newspapers certainly will be a great treat; one feels the lack of those things, and the multitude of publications we have had in such abundance in England. The whole world is so full of movement and interests. It is a trial not to know what is going on. Only one newspaper have I seen since I have been in Africa!'

Anna immensely impressed the Africans with her ability to read and to sew and use scissors, but people were rather wary of 'Book' - the Bible - presumably because they had not seen a book before. Her journal and some letters record very vividly many of the events of the early weeks and months at Ibadan. On Whit-Sunday, May 15$^{th}$, Anna wrote, ' I think you might not have been uninterested if you could have seen a certain Anna to-day, with a large mixed-up class of men and women on the ground, with her four little boys, who are with her every day, clinging to her, each trying to be nearest at this afternoon school. You must remember they are cramped for room. As I sat on my chair, one little black fellow had clasped my arm with both his hands, another every now and then nearly resting his chin on my shoulder, the other two sitting close at my feet ; and then such a burst of voices after me repeated the Lord's Prayer in Yoruba, and then two of the Commandments.

The affection of these people is very great, and in these four boys it is remarkable; if a fly comes near me they push it away. I have had a little fever in the week, so did not come out of my room all day. They were wandering about quite disconsolate, and one of them went in the evening to Olubi, with tearful eyes, saying he could not find Missis all day; and when I came out the next day they were so delighted.'

'May 26$^{th}$: I have had many visitors this week, particularly women. Their tenderness over me is touching; if they see me hot, they will fan me; if I look tired, they want me to lie down. I have had much talk with them, through my little maid Susanna (the daughter of a Christian convert who had come with them from

Yoruba ladies

Abeokuta); they do indeed receive us with joy and gladness, and we have many regular attendants on Sunday. They are quite beginning to understand that it is a holy day with us, and I feel sure some are trying to give up Sunday occupation. I am still somewhat of a curiosity, the novelty has not yet worn off, and .our house is pretty well surrounded all day long. I like to feel that, though they have come to look at me and my possessions, they go away having heard the good tidings we have come here to bring; and we only long and pray that they may receive that blessed message of salvation into their hearts. But we are on uncultivated ground, and our work at present, by God's help, is to break up the fallow ground.

It has been a lovely cool day, after rain nearly all night, and some hours this morning. The sun has not peeped out once, so that at about three o'clock we went out, Mr. Kefer too, all on horseback. The town is built on a tremendous hill; we wanted to get to the top, to see its extent, and a wonderful sight it is, myriads of houses on every side. A queer and rugged pathway we had often to travel, but I have no fear now with my good little horse. We went also through different parts of the town, to various markets; they are a pretty sight, with their native productions, but oh, the noise! We were surrounded all the way by hundreds, with open eyes and mouths. Some made music, after their fashion, and sang and shouted. Many who had visited us at our house were prepared with an extra welcome. Kola-nuts were given me and I might have had many things.'

'May 29th: Another Sabbath day hath reached its close. We have had nice services, many people, and very attentive; and some having come for several Sundays, bringing new ones with them, is very encouraging. We have now a nice little day school. Some having come very regularly, I gave them blue shirts yesterday, and it was a pretty sight this morning to be greeted by nine blue boys. I have also now four children given me, but as our house is small, and they like to go home at the end of the day, we let them. They are here early enough in the morning; a little boy and girl of [the chief] Olumloyo's; a boy whose father had been quite an enemy of ours; and a little boy without parents, the brother of our schoolmaster. Though he is so young he has been nicely taught, and is quite a help in the school. I feel I have indeed a little charge, but a precious one, and desire that a blessing may be given, that I may have grace and strength to train them up for God, and that they may walk in the right way. I only wish you could take a peep at my little group.'

The children of Chief Olumloyo were a girl, Yejide, of about six and a boy, Akielle, aged four. On their first day at the Mission all was well until sunset when the little girl was desperate to go home and eventually said, 'Akielle, we must not stay. Don't you know that when it gets dark the white people kill and eat the black?' So they went home each night. After a few days Akielle stayed the night and from then on happily made the Mission House his home.

'June 8th: Last week I had to doctor and nurse both my dear husband and Mr. Kefer; they were quite down with fever. It is such a curious malady with them, and comes so frequently; they get ill quickly, and are very ill for a few days, and then suddenly they are up again, and enjoying food. I do not mean to say that I am exempted altogether, but it seems to be different. I get hot and languid, lie down, and keep quite still, and as cool as I can, take quinine, and am soon up again: but they are so cold, they want blankets, and no one knows what, and are far more ill, and much oftener. I cannot say how thankful I am to be so well; tired enough I am by night. My children and housekeeping and visitors keep me going all day. I almost fear for writing, drawing seems out of the question; however, as I get more and more used to it, I shall more cleverly manage my time.'

Having had years of experience with children in Lowestoft, Anna discovered that African children were not so different in spite of the way in which they were brought up. However, she had to adjust her ideas in order to get them to conform to what she considered was acceptable behaviour. She wrote 'We know children are a great care and trouble at home, and can imagine that they would be rather more so in this country, having been under no control, and coming all at once into such a different life. Washing every morning, for instance, is passing strange to them; once or twice a week is the outside of what they think necessary, and why we want them ever to be quiet and silent is equally strange. They are beginning to comprehend that they must be quiet at family prayers. Nothing composes them so much as music. We always sing a hymn with the harmonium at prayers, with which they are delighted. But though decidedly a care, and no slight trouble, I would not for anything be without them; they will lose their wildness in time, and they are so affectionate.

Akielle is very high spirited, but has a most loving heart. He often comes and throws his little arms round me, exclaiming: "My mother thou art!" But he is also extremely passionate. The other day he was beating a boy bigger than himself tremendously. I interfered, and he lifted up his hand at me; then I had to punish him. He only said he would go home. I said, "Very well, Akielle, go; good-bye for ever." He burst into tears: "O no! I will never leave my Iya!" and he was quite inconsolable till received into favour. They are all happy enough, and are a real pleasure to us, and often rouse us a little, if we are inclined to be flat or weary.'

Anna had acquired a horse which she used for going on shopping rides round the town. Sadly, on June 16th she wrote, 'I had a fall from my horse on Monday last. I was accidentally pushed from a narrow pathway, by a boy, down a half-filled hole. I was thrown under it, and I quite expected broken limbs, yet, thanks to our gracious Preserver, no harm came near me.' When this accident happened it was thought to be of little consequence however it may have been the cause of later problems. For the next couple of weeks Anna and David were both unwell.

'July 6th: Since I last wrote I have been very ill; a sharp attack of fever, brought on, doubtless, from anxiety and want of rest; but I am thankful to be about again, though weak. The good hand of my God hath been over me, and I have had the tenderest care from my still suffering husband. He is, I trust, recovering, but very, very slowly; the alarming symptoms have passed over, but he is intensely weak; it is such a comfort to hear him speak this evening a little above a whisper. He has indeed been brought to the edge of the grave, and is so altered I think you would hardly know him. I have sometimes almost been inclined to ask, Can it be he? It must be long before he quite recovers; but I am so thankful that there is a prospect of this blessing. The interest and sympathy of the people have been very touching …'

Although there were local people who were medical practitioners, how much medical knowledge they had is not known. They may have been very perplexed by the periods of illness suffered by the missionaries. Anna told how 'Our young warrior, Olumloyo, has come every day, and has been truly heart-broken; he told me I must pray much for my husband. The orange season is just over, we could not get one in the market; I mentioned it to Olumloyo, when he sent his servants to the farms, but they came back without any. He was very sorry, "Yet I must have some," he said; and he mounted his horse and galloped off to several farms, and brought back eleven, with great delight. He sat by the bed and saw the dear patient devour one almost greedily; the young chief was so pleased that tears filled his eyes. My husband tried to thank him, Olumloyo lifted up his hand, exclaiming, "Don't speak: I am too glad." He came this afternoon and saw my husband on the sofa; he was very much pleased, and told Olubi that many people would be so glad to have the white man well again, that there would be much rejoicing when he could once more get out; they would fire many guns, he himself would give a whole cask of powder.'

'July 10th, Sunday: I must close this day with a few words with my friends. I have been at school twice, and at one service; during the other service, I stayed with my husband. He had a comfortable morning, though rather a trying afternoon; but after tea he revived much, and said he should like our usual singing. So now for the gathering. I only wish you could have seen it. Mr. Hinderer on the sofa, Mr. Kefer near him, our Christian visitor on a chair; in the wide doorway, on the ground, his daughter Martha, a girl of ten years, our two men Simon and Jacob, our horseman, cook's wife, and one or two of Mr. Kefer's servants; I at the harmonium, with two little lamps fixed in wine glasses for convenience sake; on a long bench, close behind me, Olubi, Benjamin, Susanna, schoolmaster, carpenter, and cook.

Two of my boys, who are very fond of singing, and could keep their eyes open, stood one on each side of me, sometimes listening, and sometimes putting in a few sounds; and then we had a hearty singing truly. These people have the art of catching an air quickly, and are able to follow music; and they sang the collect for the day, the 7th Sunday after Trinity, beautifully; then we had the Lowestoft hymn-book box and we finished with "Praise God, from whom all blessings flow." Afterwards I pointed to the dear pictures [of Mr. and Mrs. Cunningham] hanging over the harmonium, and said to them there was no sight would delight that dear lady and gentleman much more than the present; and told them of our Sunday evenings at home. They were much interested, and said they were glad they had some one who liked to sing with them in Africa, and who had such a nice instrument. It did us all good; my husband was cheered, and to me it was like a refreshing pool in the midst of a dry and thirsty land. My spirit had been sad and weary…'

'August 20th: I am again permitted to write to you, after a most severe sickness. What a wonderful thing, in the midst of all, not to have been prevented sending something every mail. With a weak hand I wrote a few lines last month, telling you I had inflammation in the lungs; after that was gone I was much worse for three whole weeks, touched nothing but water, tea, a little raspberry vinegar, and in very sinking moments, once or twice, I think they gave me weak brandy and water. A whole week they had looked for my end; several times I seemed almost gone; I feel I was prayed back to life, for once I was quite conscious, and felt the journey of life ending, and that I should be with my Saviour, the body of clay sleeping the sleep of death, with those who so lately have been taken from amongst us, till the resurrection morn. My poor afflicted husband had sent a special messenger to Abeokuta on horseback, to request their prayers, and on the day he arrived, they appointed an hour in the evening for special pleading on my behalf; and that self-same hour, after an intensely suffering day, I became easier and better; God listened to their cry, and while they were speaking He graciously answered. Here I am, weaker indeed, but getting on day by day, through God s infinite mercy, and oh, I trust, for some good purpose to my own soul, and the souls of others. Everyone says this is a great encouragement for the future, that I am become more Africanised and shall be less and less affected by the climate.'

By August the number of children in the school had grown to sixteen and their parents were obviously appreciative. On 16th August Anna wrote: 'I have had a treat to-day, my sixteen school-children to dinner. They were so good while I was ill that I wished to give them a treat when well again. We gave them a large bowl of palaver sauce, with a huge quantity of beaten yams ; afterwards pictures, then an examination as to what they had learned in school, a little talk, which was followed by a good game at ball, then each had a present from my toy-box, such as a knife, or a box for cowries. They were delighted indeed, and after a little more eating of agidi, and an orange, I sent them off by six o'clock, and then we had visits from their parents to thank us.

It was a real pleasure to me to see them getting on so nicely, four of them now begin to read the Yoruba Testament; all have learned *Watts' Little Catechism*, which has been translated, and the commandments; two are also learning the English primer. They extremely like to learn English sentences, and names of things. I am always saluted by them with "Good-morning, Ma'am." When walking out with my four boys, they tell me Yoruba names of things, and then ask for the English in return, and they remember the English name much better than I do the Yoruba.'

*Watts Little Catechism* was a book for children, giving the names of people mentioned in the Bible and explaining who they were. It was written by Isaac Watts, nowadays more famous for the wonderfully inspirational hymns he wrote.

The way in which the children were responding to their teaching never ceased to delight Anna who wrote: 'My four boys go on most comfortably together, and I am quite encouraged about them. Akielle, the youngest of them, fell asleep once during the Sunday evening singing, and was carried to his mat. The next morning he came to me, saying, "Iya, I did not say my prayers last night, shall I now?" I am teaching them to sew and to knit, for I want occupation for them, as the school only lasts from nine to twelve. From five to six we generally walk, play ball, and all sorts of things and Iya must play with them as well as work; their great delight is truly doubled when my husband will run and let them catch him. So with one thing and another, you can believe, I have not much idle time.

We have very pleasant Sunday evenings over the Noah's ark, or Mrs. [Hannah] Buxton's beautiful Scripture pictures. After that, the whole household come in for singing. The children are now very good at church. On Sunday, in speaking on the vanity and helplessness of idols, Mr. Hinderer quoted the Psalm, "They have mouths and speak not," the boys burst out laughing, and said it was true, very true; this was not very decorous truly, but it showed they were attentive. Our palm leaf shed has stood the rainy season very well, and has been nicely filled. We recognize a few regular attendants, and all like Sunday school.'

For Anna and David to have English visitors was always exciting. 'October 1st: Mr. and Mrs. Townsend [from Abeokuta] came to pay us a visit; we were very glad to have them with us in our little dwelling, which I was almost inclined to think must be made of something elastic, for we packed in very comfortably, and were truly glad of a little white society. The people were astonished, and frightened too, to see five white people together; and when we all went out it was amusing and fatiguing enough. We are still much surrounded by visitors, who wonder at all they see; they think me much more industrious than I think myself; they laugh to see me write, and wonder that I can read so many books and the wonderful things I can do with a needle and scissors....My little black boys are my greatest occupation, so that they and their doings, or mine with them, are interspersed through everything, for I am mother, playfellow, teacher....'

Although Anna and David were content with their first home, it had many shortcomings and was not reliably weatherproof. Something much more substantial was needed. A further plot of land was granted to them by the chiefs and plans for a new house were soon formulated. 'November 19th: This has been an eventful week. On Monday, the 14th, we commenced building the wall of our compound; the foundation of our house also is laid, and the corners built up a little way. The first floor will be about six or seven feet high, which will be used for stores, and we shall mount up, and have three good rooms and smaller rooms made in the piazza. I can hardly fancy I am to have such comfort, yet it is with a loose hand one holds it. We have a class on Saturday for candidates for baptism, some of our own servants not being baptized.'

In December Anna recorded that they had decided that it was necessary for the young man who had been the schoolmaster to join David and Mr. Kefer in going out preaching the Gospel in the town and walking about and talking to people as that was the major way of spreading their message. Another schoolmaster would be needed and so it was decided that their very capable Olubi should become the schoolmaster. 'We have made a sacrifice, and given up our faithful Olubi for the school. It is a sacrifice, for he was the only one in the house we could look to for everything, but he is a good creature, and very ready to give a helping hand when school is over, and I believe he will make an excellent schoolmaster, he is so fond of children, and has so much heart in everything.

PREACHING IN A YORUBA VILLAGE.

The dear children are very ready to receive instruction, and it was quite a grief to them when they had a few days holiday; they were not a little delighted to have some lessons with me. It is so interesting to watch their opening minds. I asked one of my little boys if he liked to sit down with me. "O yes, indeed I do," was his answer. "Because I learn so many nice things here, and you, Iya, love me, and are so kind to me." I asked, "Do you love God?" "Yes, because He is so great and good." "Do you love Jesus?" "Yes, yes" and he ended with saying, "I want to hear more of Jesus, and know more."

## 1854

From the weather point of view the winter months from December to March were a great trial. It was when the dry and dusty West African trade wind, called the harmattan, blew across from the Sahara into the Gulf of Guinea. Early in the New Year, illness affected both Mr. Kefer and Anna who wrote: 'January 20th: I have again been laid very low, in consequence, in some measure I doubt not, of the late anxious nursing of Mr. Kefer. When a fellow-labourer is brought down to the gates of death, all one's endeavours, anxieties, and sympathies are called forth, and one feels the effects afterwards, the body and the nerves suffer; but we are also passing through the trying season, the harmattan. I have had lingering fever; I feel very weak, and unable to do anything; the bed and the sofa are very much my resources, and I cannot get round as I usually do; however, we hope on, and are as cheerful as is possible with a weary body of clay. My dear husband is always cheerful and cheering, never despairing, never doubting, never distrusting; even in the dark cloudy day he passes on with all his burdens. I must confess I have had a low time, and have been walking on the dark and shady side of life. I have felt "what am I?" and could not bear to be looked at by the people who are all day watching us. I felt they must think me a very lazy white woman, but yet I think my pale thin face and tottering limbs must have been an excuse for me; however, the happiest way of thinking was that this was my time of education and preparation for future work, and so I endeavoured to lie passive, only seeking to be made entirely resigned to do or to suffer my Father's will.'

There were encouraging signs that the Africans were being impressed by the Christian message that they were hearing. 'February 21st: Now I must tell you some of our encouragements, not perhaps conversions, but something approaching thereto. Many people in this town are not exactly slaves, but are in pawn. Their parents have wanted money, perhaps, and have given their children as security, so that after a time the one in pawn has to work so many days for his master without any reward, and the remaining days, according to the master's generosity, for himself, to earn enough for his entire food and clothing. A poor fellow in this position came to church whenever his master's working day did not fall upon a Sunday, and became so interested in all he heard, that he said he could not work on Sunday, he should beg his master to give him that day always, and he would give him one of his own week days. Now that is something like self-denial, is it not?

One of our church builders also is full of enquiry, and says his heart cannot sit down, he cannot follow his past fashion, neither can he take white man's fashion altogether.

Our sawyer is a heathen from Abeokuta, whom we begged to come and saw for us. His friends sent for him the other day to go and make the usual 'country fashion' with them. He sent them word "No". Since he had been here he had seen and heard things so different. They begged, they threatened, he said he could not help what they did, but he could not join with them in their heathen worship. He attends church regularly and Sunday school too, and is eager to learn to read.

A country priest who has troubled us, and tried to prejudice others against us, came the other day, saying, "I get no peace, I want to give my heart to God."

A famous priestess came to convert us, but returned to think for herself, and has had some serious talks with Olubi. So we are greatly encouraged in our work.'

All was not well however for some of those who came to the Mission. They heard about one little girl who was put in chains for three days of punishment because she had been there, and about other people – usually women – who were severely persecuted and even tortured for showing any interest in the activities of the Christians.

While the missionary work was continuing and the building of the new house was steadily progressing, Anna was increasingly unwell. This was a real dilemma. What should be done?

# Chapter 4 Settling into the permanent home and the establishment of the Kudeti Mission 1854-56

During the early weeks of 1854 Anna was very unwell, so after much persuasion it was decided that she should go to stay at the Abeokuta Mission for a good rest and recuperation. David went with her but could not stay as he needed to supervise and be involved in the building of the new house, which was becoming an increasing necessity. David had become a very skilled craftsman before training for the priesthood. Later Anna wrote: 'The kindness and hospitality of Mr. and Mrs. Townsend are never to be forgotten; I enjoyed being under their roof and with them, and was much interested in all that is going on around them. Mrs. Townsend cared for me as a sister…'

From Abeokuta Anna wrote in a letter to England in April: 'It was by no means easy to get away from home, and I felt it much, the dear boys were so sorrowful. They came a little way on the road with us after many promises, before leaving the house, that I would not go to England, when I got as far as Abeokuta; and when we halted under a tree, to take a final leave for a time, I got off my horse, and if you could just have seen it, you would have said, African children have hearts, and very tender loving ones too. One of my boys, about ten or eleven years old, could bear it no longer; he laid his head on my side and sobbed, and as he could get the words out, said, "Go, dear Iya, and make haste back" and then turned his face and steps towards home. You will not think me egotistical, but this I do think, if I am come to Africa for nothing else, I have found the way to a few children's hearts, and if spared, and I have health and strength, I think I shall not, with God s blessing, find it very difficult to do something with them.

…My boys that I have now, would never tell me an untruth, or touch a cowry or any thing they should not. This is truly wonderful for heathen boys, brought up all their lives, hitherto, in the midst of every kind of deceit. Dear fellows, I feel sure the love and blessing of God is over them and their young hearts are opening, I humbly trust, to receive Him as their only God and Saviour, and I hope I am very thankful to have found favour amongst them. I must add, though I may fill a larger place in their affections, having more to do with them, yet my husband, shares in it considerably.'

On May 9th Anna wrote: 'I long to be at home again, and grudge every hour from my beloved Ibadan; only the assurance and advice of everybody, that I ought to have some sort of change, could have moved me. Tomorrow we hope to be on our way to Ibadan, and we go with joy and gladness of heart. I cannot be thankful enough to be able to return with renewed health and strength .....and I certainly feel there is no place in all Africa like that home.'

'Ibadan, May 14th: Yesterday I reached my loved Ibadan home, amidst a hearty greeting from the dear boys. Laniyono, who was the most sorrowful when I left, gave a shriek of delight, and sprang into my arms, with his legs round my waist, hanging there to his heart's content, shouting and making the oddest remarks you ever heard; that I was never to go away again, seemed to be a certainty to his mind. But a tinge of bitterness is generally mixed with every cup, so I found here. Two of my boys had been taken away by their parents in my absence: Adelotan is not allowed to appear anywhere, but Abudu came at once to see me. I put my hand on his shoulder, and he burst into a flood of tears. "O Iya, it is not me, it is not me, it is my father who has done it." Poor child! I could only soothe and calm him, and bid him be patient. I believe he will soon get leave from his father to come back.

Our new house, after all the toil in building it promises to possess all the comfort we could expect or desire in this country; it is watertight! has a good-sized sitting and bed-room, white-washed walls, and a good iron roof; comfortable piazzas, and all very airy, and as cool as anything can be in Africa, which was my principal desire. It is wonderful what my dear husband has achieved in my absence, and now he rejoices to have his wife in it, and so does she to be there. We pray that a rich blessing may be given us with it, and that though we have the comfort of a dwelling, we may never forget that this is not our home, but a tent pitched for the day.'

The house built at Kudeti in 1854 (from the collection of Mrs. Dolapo Falomo)

The new home, which was virtually a creation of an English gentleman's house with its provision for numerous members of staff, had an outside staircase. Was this on wheels? It is difficult to envisage. Soon Anna and David were most delighted to receive a visit from Bale, the head chief. Anna wrote: 'May 17th: Bale, the head chief, paid us a special visit to-day. He came in great state, with drums and various strange instruments of music, with his host of attendants, singing men and singing women. He marvelled greatly at our house, and could not imagine how it was made. He was quite alarmed to think of mounting the steps; but with my husband pulling, and others pushing, we got him up. I stood at the top to receive him, in his mass of silks and velvets; he very graciously took my hand, and we walked into the room, at the sight of which he gave a great shout and wondered; he then took a fancy to the sofa, and sat there. We admitted upstairs his wives, his eldest son, and a few of his great people, and then were obliged to move away the steps, or the house, strong as it is, must have broken down with the mass of people. We gave him and those in the room with him, a little refreshment, English bread, biscuits, and a few raisins.

They looked at the bedroom, and all the things in both rooms. Bale was extremely amused to see himself in the looking-glass. I took the women by themselves; the washing-stand attracted their attention, so I washed my hands to show them the use of it. My soap was wonderful and that I wiped my hands after I had washed them was a thing unheard of. But they took it into their heads to follow my example, and all hands must touch the soap, and go into the water, and there was a fine splashing, and a pretty towel, for the indigo dye comes off their clothes so very much, that I believe the towel will be blue and white for ever. At last we got into a state of composure again, and all being quiet, Mr. Hinderer made a little speech, telling Bale how glad we were to see him, why we built the house, and what brought us to this country.'

'May 22nd: A woman of about fifty years of age came to me. I noticed her in church, two or three Sundays before I went away, and again she was there yesterday. She brought with her a fowl, and corn to feed it with, and yams; she put them before me as a present, and said, "Iya, all my life I have served the devil; he has been my god; but he never gave me peace in my heart. My husband was stolen away by war, the devil did not help me; my children all died, the devil could not help me; but since you white people have come, I have heard the words of the Great God, which we never heard before, and they are sweet to me. I want to hear more, and to walk in the right road, for it has been a wrong road all my life." She has thrown her husband's images into the water. After our last words, "God bless you, and give you peace in your heart!" she uttered a most fervent and hearty "Amen." As it is the constant practice to take fowls, cowries, and other offerings to their gods, I thought it necessary to tell her we did not desire she should bring a full hand to us: she said she knew it, but begged we would accept her little present, to make her happy. I had a little chintz bag hanging up, with not a handful of cowries in it; she would not have had cowries as a payment on any account, but the bag she could not refuse; such a possession she never thought to have, and she went off with it greatly delighted.'

'June 22nd: We are both in very good health and both as busy as bees. A day is never long enough for me; a great deal falls to my share, and I can fancy no one more happy than myself in being equal to it in bodily power. My dear little boys give me great comfort and satisfaction. I must tell you one story about them. (The way that we teach children Bible stories was also Anna's way.) On Sunday week we had studied and talked over the picture of Dorcas. Yesterday evening they came to me for their prayers in my bedroom, and particularly noticed the beautiful figure I have of dear Mrs. Fry, which stands on my dressing-table, and which always seems to say, "Be ye followers of them who through faith and patience inherit the Promises." They asked me who it was, I told them; and, as far as I could, of her love to all people, especially the afflicted ones, the prisoner, the slave, &c. They listened attentively till big tears stood in the eyes of one. I then asked if they had ever heard of any one being so kind. One said she was like Dorcas, full of good deeds; another that she was like their own Iya, who could leave her own country and friends and come to them, and love little black boys and girls and people so much. No, I said, there was One whose example Mrs. Fry followed, who did far more than either Dorcas or Iya. A little fellow, the youngest of all, exclaimed, "It is Jesus, Iya means, who went about always doing good, and then gave His life for all." Do you know I thought it was worth while to come to Africa, only to hear this from little lips which, such a short time ago, were taught senseless words over wood, and stone, and charms.'

Elizabeth Fry

Although no doubt Anna and David were prepared for the unexpected, one wonders whether they anticipated opening their home to the numerous abandoned children they came across. 'July 11th: Early this morning the wife of one of our native agents and our young schoolmaster went into the town, to accompany a friend on the road to Ijaye. On their way back they saw a little boy, not three years old, looking cold, starved, and filthy; they went towards the poor little thing, who said, "Era mi, - Buy me, buy me; I want to go home with you." On enquiring they found that he was the child of a slave; the mother was sold many months ago, far away; the master of the house where the child was is gone to war, and so what was everybody's charge became nobody's. One man, who did just feed him for a time, got tired of him, and said he had enough to do to feed himself, for he also was a slave; so the poor child was cast out into the street. No one would dare to take him, lest they should be charged with stealing a slave, and for three moons, as the people say, he had been there, night and day; a few days more, and he must have died. All the food he got would be a bit of agidi, or corn, which would be thrown to him by passers-by, as you would to a fowl. Olubi talked with the people, but they only said they could not help it and wondered any one should care about a little slave.

Mr. Hinderer immediately returned with Olubi. Meantime a woman in the yard had washed the child, and shaved his head; he had also been abundantly oiled, and rubbed over with canewood. Mr. Hinderer talked with the people, and at last they said, "Take him if you like; if he live, he live; if he die, well; no one make palaver with you;" so my husband hired a woman to carry him on her back, and bring him to me; and here he is, a pretty looking little child, but with a countenance so full of sorrow, and he is a poor miserable skeleton. After a little more washing, I put on him a frock, and wrapped him in a warm cloth, which he seemed thoroughly to enjoy. I took him on my lap, and he seemed quite at home there. We gave him a little food, which he ate most greedily. We must be very careful about his food for some little time, or he would kill himself with eating. He soon fell fast asleep in my arms. As I was watching his sweet sleep, "Take this child and nurse it for me, and I will give thee thy wages seemed to ring in my ears", and we do receive him as a precious little charge. May I be enabled to bring him up for God. He may be a bright and shining light. I wish his poor mother could know he was well taken care of.'

The above is interesting. It is noticeable that neither David nor Olubi picked up the child. It was obviously not something that men did. Also, Anna says that she 'put on him a frock'. Young European children, both boys and girls, wore frocks in the 19th century.

'July 20th: The little boy improves in health, but is not very good-tempered. The poor dear child has all the effects of being starved and unkindly treated, and at present all he can think of is eating. The other day I played with him a little, and he condescended to look at me. On my saying, I think you like me a little better to-day, the reply was, "What will you give me to eat?"

This dear child has hardly a mind to appreciate kindness, having only known cruelty and oppression.'

During the last few months work had also been started on the new church as the first church had been badly battered by tornadoes and its roof of grass and palm leaves ripped away. The new church, even though still roofless, was gladly brought into use on July 23rd.

THE CHURCH AT IBADAN.

Anna wrote: 'Now we have the outward walls, and we pray God to build up a spiritual house within. Grant that the sons and daughters of Ibadan may become polished corners of the temple! Hear Thou from heaven Thy dwelling-place, and send out Thy grace and Thy blessing! It is curious to watch people listening for the first time to the new tidings, a little gentle remark, then an expression of doubt, then such a hearty Amen.'

When one of Anna's pupils was no longer attending the Mission, David went to discover what had happened to him. 'August 13$^{th}$: My husband was going to visit Laniyono, who had been taken away by his father a week ago, at his father's house to-day, but, hearing his voice as in prayer, he waited, and heard him pour forth his petitions most earnestly, "I want to love Thee, I want to be Thy child." When his voice ceased, he went in, and there he found the dear child alone with his little heathen brothers and sisters; and, as he came away, they burst forth in singing an English hymn, which he had evidently taught them in the week. I think we may trust that a work of grace is commenced in that dear boy's heart, and hope his being at home for a short time may not be for harm, but for good. I went in, a few days since, and they were all gathered round their meal; he was standing up, and, with eyes shut and hands folded, repeated the grace we had taught him, and all the children said, "Amen."

'August 20th: Another bright Sunday! How I love to feel bright and happy on Sundays. They have been such blessed days to me, and I am so thankful to find their brightness returning. There is so much more peace and quietness round about us now; our neighbours seem to feel it is a holy day with us, and those who do not yet join in keeping it with us are ashamed to be seen by us doing their own work. No one thinks of coming to offer any thing for sale in our yard.'

'On the 5th of October a real treat was given us in the arrival of a beautiful box of things from Lady Buxton. It was such a feast that the children were wild with delight, whilst I myself was not much less so. The children were greatly pleased with the playthings, and not less so with Iya's new dress. They do so curiously enjoy any new thing for me, and fail not to admire it abundantly. Even when the letters arrive, they give a loud shout, and go singing about, "Iya gets book from her father and mother, sisters and brothers, and friends, far far away. Oh, it is good!" followed by more shouts; and then they creep up for the empty envelopes, which is their share of the feast. The beautiful Scripture puzzle and Scripture pictures I hid until Sunday evening; and how I wish our dear friends in England could have seen the children's interest when I explained them. I did not give them anything until the 14th, the second anniversary of our wedding, when we made a feast for all those who were in our little day school. I gave each of the girls one of the nice little handkerchiefs and a pretty pin to fasten it, to their very great delight; and they looked so neat and tidy the next Sunday at church. The boys had their share of guns and tops, but a pencil and piece of paper is their crowning pleasure. Anything that gives pleasure to the children has a soothing comfortable effect on my mind. It smooths the ripples which arise on daily life.'

Hannah - Lady Buxton - was the widow of Sir Thomas Fowell Buxton and a sister of Richenda Cunningham. One of her granddaughters - Ellen Creighton née Buxton - described how when they had holidays with their grandmother at Northrepps she used to enlist their help in collecting toys and other gifts and then packing them in parcels to be sent in the mail to Mrs Hinderer for her children in Africa.

November was very memorable as it was when they had a visit from Bishop Vidal. Anna wrote: 'The month of November is marked by the visit of our good and valued Bishop Vidal. On the 9th November he arrived in Ibadan, accompanied by Archdeacon Graf, Mr. Townsend and Dr. Irving; so that, including our three selves, we were seven white people in Ibadan, quite an event! On Sunday the Bishop confirmed nine of our people, and delivered, through an interpreter, a most striking address. On Monday evening he addressed the confirmed and our native helpers. It was so solemn, so tender, so impressive: it is indelibly stamped on our minds. The visit of our beloved and honoured Bishop, his kind interest, and tender sympathy in us and our work, have been as a refreshing draught in a dry and thirsty land. We rejoice and give thanks that such a head has been granted us; his brilliant example must have some effect upon us all.'

Among other people who had become welcome visitors to the Mission was Dr. Irving. He was a surgeon in the Royal Navy and also an intrepid traveller and plantsman. In December he and David set off to the country of the Ijebu which lay between Ibadan and the coast and had previously been inaccessible to Europeans.

The visit was at the invitation of the king who had requested that the white man of Ibadan should come to meet him 'face to face'. Diplomacy certainly required that the invitation should be accepted and it was obviously an opportunity not to be missed.

Anna wrote: 'My husband left on Friday. I felt parting with him, but was glad he should go on such an errand, and trust they may have much blessing in their journey. It will be a wonderful blow to slavery and all sorts of cruelties, if the banner of the Cross be erected and light and salvation be proclaimed and accepted there. So here I am all alone. I think it says much for a town in Africa, of one hundred thousand inhabitants, that one white woman can be left alone, in perfect safety, and with no fear.'

While David was away Anna grasped another opportunity. It was to visit the Iyalode of Ibadan and she wrote in her journal; 'These Yoruba people have some very nice arrangements about their form of government. I found out that there was an Iyalode or mother of the town, to whom all the women's palavers (disputes) are brought before they are taken to the king. She is, in fact, a sort of queen, a person of much influence, and looked up to with much respect. I sent my messenger to her, to tell her I should like to visit her. She sent word she should be delighted; so on Monday the 18th, I went with the children and we found a most respectable motherly looking person, surrounded by her attendants and people, in great order, and some measure of state. I told them why I came to this country, and entreated them to come and hear the Word of God for themselves, and send their children to us to be taught. We two Iyas made strong friendship, by my giving, and her receiving, a fine velvet head-tie, and a silk bag; and the lady settled that we were to be the two mothers of the town, she the Iyalode still, and I the Iyalode for fun, the white Iyalode. I then spoke to myriads of children; and after sundry shouts, a variety of blessings, and divers shakes of my hand which seemed to be a great honour and privilege, I at last got away. Three days after my visit, the Iyalode sent to salute me, begging me to accept from her a goat, and a calabash of yams, to make a feast for my children and people.'

What did this Iyalode who lived in such grandeur think of Anna, arriving with her entourage of lively chattering yet well disciplined children? What was the name of the Iyalode? Anna did not say. Was she Efusetan Aniwura, a remarkable lady of tremendous wealth created by her amazing flair for trade and commerce? She was a very powerful person in Ibadan in the 1850s, 1860s and 1870s who lived in a very grand style and whose success was the envy of her male business rivals. If she was Efusetan Aniwura, it would have been a meeting of two very contrasting passionate women. One was determined never to lose an opportunity to build up her commercial empire. The other was determined never to lose an opportunity to sow the seeds of the Kingdom of Heaven. Their mutual respect and friendship would have been an important part of international diplomacy. Their legacies to Ibadan were very different.

## 1855

'January3rd Wednesday: I went with all our people far on the Ijebu road, to meet my husband, but alas, he did not come. We were a nice large party, Odehinde joined us, which was very kind, and shewed real love to his minister by losing a whole day's labour for the pleasure of meeting him. We were all much disappointed.'

'January 4th: At 4 A.M., a man arrived with letters to say my husband expected to be back on Thursday or Friday, but this afternoon, about half-past two, to our great joy, he arrived with Dr. Irving, tired enough, but delighted to be home. I do enjoy having D. safe at home again, after such a journey of mercies, and such a successful one. We thank Thee, Lord of heaven and earth! Dr. Irving left us on the following Monday.'

'January 19th: Now, alas, I have my tale of sorrow to tell. I told you my beloved husband had gone on a journey, he returned on Thursday afternoon, the 4th instant, worn and tired, but he soon got quite refreshed. On the following Monday he was so cheerful, talking of the pleasure of being at home and making plans for the future for visiting every part of this immense town.

In the afternoon he was rather feverish, and went to lie down, but from that bed he has never been up since, except for an hour or so from restlessness, or because he thought himself better.'

There followed a time of desperate crisis. David's fever became extremely severe. Anna, usually so calm, became extremely distraught with the exhaustion of nursing and the anxiety of wondering whether this was the end for David. If it was not, would he recover enough to be able to continue his life's work? She felt completely helpless and was also tormented with wondering what she would do if left alone in this foreign land. She sent a messenger to her friends at Abeokuta Mission and to her great relief the Reverend Samuel Crowther arrived on 21st January. Although David appeared to be terminally ill Samuel Crowther had the skill to pull him through and he gradually recovered. On 11th February he was even able to preach again at the Sunday service.

The next delivery of mail brought very sad news. It was of the death of yet another of the little band who had sailed together from England two years before – Bishop Vidal who had been such a tower of strength to them.

The progress the children were making always encouraged Anna, especially in the drawing lessons. She wrote: 'March 30th: We stood by a beautiful brook, where short palm-trees were growing luxuriantly; the children were much struck in comparing these with a dry and withered one further off. I just mentioned their having learned a Psalm with me, which they might remember while looking at the two trees; they at once thought of the first, and we had such an eager earnest talk. They went on comparing things around us with scripture illustrations. We gathered wild flowers on the way, and seeing a bush with exquisite green leaves, I sent them to gather some. When I overtook them, I found them with most solemn faces and sighing….. The bush was full of thorns, one held up his bleeding hands, and asked, "Iya, could it be thorns like these they made Jesus a crown of?"

Being always conscious of building relationships with local people especially the women, Anna recorded: 'I have lately commenced visiting in the compounds within walking distance. I am warmly received, the best mat is spread on the ground, upon which I sit as comfortably as if I had never been used to a chair, and we have a friendly conversation. I tell them why I have come to this country, of God's house being open for them, of God's love to them and to me and sometimes I ask them if they would not like to hear one little word from God's Book, and they are sure to say "Mo fe, I like." Then, I make them repeat some text after me.'

Early in May further sad news reached them - their dear friend Dr. Irving had died. Anna wrote: 'May 4th: I look at our little church, and the fence which is erecting around it to enclose a space for burials, and think, though no white person sleeps there yet, how soon there may be? How soon I may lie there? May we only be ready; and if so, through the mercy and righteousness of a Saviour, when the work appointed for us to do is done, and the summons is given, I do feel I could gladly exchange the tumults of earth, for the pleasures of heaven. The weakness, frailty, and suffering of the poor body, the imperfect state in which one now is, the constant feeling, when I would do good, evil is present with me, all make me long for the time when we shall serve our God and Saviour without a veil between, without any impediment. At the same time, if it pleases God to spare us, I hope I should not only be content to live, but rejoice in it, if I may live to His honour and glory.'

Very soon after that a burial space was filled – by Mr. Kefer. Feeling quite fit, he had gone on a preaching tour but was suddenly struck down with the most severe form of yellow fever. His horse without a rider was brought back to the Mission followed by Mr. Kefer in a hammock. As he was carried into the house he smiled weakly to them but that evening as Anna and David and several others gathered round his bed in prayer he slipped away from this earthly life into life eternal. The next day he was the first person to be laid to rest in their little Kudeti churchyard.

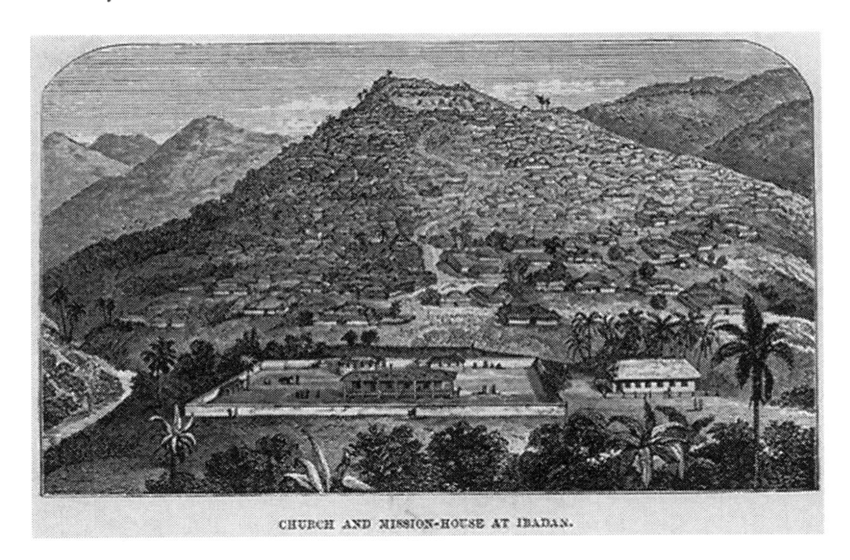

CHURCH AND MISSION-HOUSE AT IBADAN.

'Sunday, June 15th: Our one bell, the gift of the Chelsea Juvenile Association, is very refreshing; I am so reminded of the lines my Saturday class at home used to sing so prettily: "Sweetly the Sabbath bell steals on the ear."

'June 23rd: I have been gladdened this day by receiving into our house a dear bright intelligent little fellow, a slave; he is delighted with everything, asking, "What is this? And what is that?" He is very affectionate too. Once he sprang into my arms and put his arms round my neck, saying, "You won't let me be sold away, will you? For I want to stop with you", and then looking me full in the face, and laughing, he said, "You can't kiss me, because I am black, and you are white.," I gave him immediately two or three kisses, which amused him immensely.'

'Sunday, June 24th: My dear husband had the joy of admitting, by baptism, into the visible church, five converts, the Ibadan first-fruits. Our church was roofless, through the heavy gale, but in the neat and orderly place where service has been since conducted, knelt two women, two young men, and an old man, to receive the seal and sign that they to be henceforth Christ's faithful soldiers and servants. Instead of their usual blue cloths, they wore each a white one; and their countenances showed great seriousness, and a thorough understanding of the service in which they were engaged. The congregation was very good, many heathen were present, and all seemed struck with the whole service. I think I never felt such a solemn silence as there was on this occasion - many a tear glistened in a bright black eye. It was very touching and beautiful, and most encouraging. We could but think many might come forth, from among these same lookers on, to enlist under the same banner. Our Sunday congregations are increasing, and the good tidings are not without effect.'

'July 21st: A gatekeeper has sent us two fowls, two large baskets of yams, a basket of fruit for the children and some kolas especially for me. This is extremely kind, for the Matthews at the receipt of custom get nothing from us; we and our goods are allowed to go free through every gate without paying tribute, so that this present is quite a token of love. I think among the rich Africans I never saw a more affectionate heart; he wept bitterly when we sent to inform him of Mr. Kefer's death, and came himself to express his sympathy.'

'My husband wanted bamboos, which are very scarce in this town, to repair the roof of the church. He went to quite a stranger, hearing he had some, and was treated with all civility and kindness, and when he came to settling the price of them, he was content with a mere trifle; so unusual with these people, who generally want white men to pay three times as much as others; and when we sent him a little present in return for his kindness, he was so delighted, that he says the whole bamboo field is ours, and while bamboos grow, white man shall never want for any. These may seem little things to friends at home, and hardly worth putting on paper, but they are great things to us, for we hail with joy and thankfulness any sign of kind feeling and willingness to help us, knowing that when they get confidence in us, and a friendly feeling towards us, they will listen to the good word we are come to bring to them.'

'August 13th: We have had our first Christian wedding, and very nice and simple it was. We superintended the dinner; and the speeches (for Africans can make fine speeches) were surprising to me, so marked by their Christian tone. The bride and bridegroom were quite touched by them and their eyes filled with tears.'

A Christian wedding was a most significant event. For people living in a society in which polygamy was the normal way of life, for two people to commit themselves to a Christian marriage was a very major step. The Christian teaching of marriage being between one man and one woman, who promised to stay together faithfully for life, must have seemed an exceedingly strange concept. It did, in fact, present an obstacle to some prospective early converts who were living in polygamous relationships.

'Our Sunday school numbers between forty and fifty adults, all in earnest to learn, and it is surprising what progress they make in reading. They buy the translations of the Scriptures as soon as they come out, and treasure them up as gold; but by the rest of the people, till their own eyes are opened, these are looked down upon as contemptible, and are called book followers, forsakers of their forefathers and despisers of their Gods who have given them strength, power and everything. It must be remembered that here, where things are only commencing, where a book had never been seen, no one man, woman, or child, could know a letter till we came to teach them. To leave books anywhere would be useless, and worse than useless; we have to be careful not even to throw down a little piece of paper, for it would surely be taken and used as a charm.'

At the end of September David made a business trip to Lagos, leaving Anna at home. This was probably to collect his allowance and bring back a further supply of cowries. She wrote: 'October 1$^{st}$: I am so thankful for the peace and quietness which is given me. I lie down as quietly at night as if I had every earthly guard. Now this is not natural to me, but is given me by a loving God.'

'October 5th: My husband arrived today, alone and unannounced. Such a delight! I had given him up till to-morrow, but soon I heard a terrific shout from the children and people, "Babba de," and there he was! He comes well and happy, after a most pleasant visit. He is so full of delight at being at home again. But he brings the mail also, which tells of the death of our beloved friend Mrs. Cunningham. While we mourn for ourselves, it is sweet to think of that pure and beautiful spirit in the realms above, with her God and Saviour, where all is peace, and joy, and love. I love to think of her, what she was here below, and what she must be now. I feel continually what a privilege it has been to me to have had such an example and such a friend; to have lived under her roof, and to have shared her counsel, advice, and affectionate love and interest. May every thought of her make me remember the account I must give of the privileges and blessings I have enjoyed, and stimulate me to follow her example in industry, perseverance, gentleness, meekness, and every Christian grace which shone so very brightly in her. I feel, in every step of my African career, how much I owe to her and to Mr. Cunningham, which can never be told.'

'Sunday, November 9th: Eight of the dear children living with me partook of the blessed ordinance of baptism with six others. It was with peculiar interest I presented them, one by one, to their loved minister, to receive the outward and visible sign; I hope and believe they may be made partakers of the inward and spiritual grace. They were Onisaga, Akielle, Laniyono, Arubo, Elukolo, Abudu, Ogunyomi, and Mary Ann Macaulay, a child from Sierra Leone [possibly the daughter of the Revd. T.B.Macaulay – an African priest]. I dressed them all in new white clothes, with an earnest desire in my heart that they might be possessors of the robe made white in the blood of the Lamb. God, keep these little lambs of Thy fold, shield them from all evil, and accept them for Thine own, through the love of Thy Son, our Saviour!

Many of our neighbours had had a meeting, and made a solemn promise that, for a certain season, they would not allow one of their people to come near God's house. They seemed to succeed at first, but the spies carried the report of that Sunday, "It is no use we keep our people away, the white man can still do his own work and way, whatever we do: this day he has given fourteen the new name." That expression, "the new name" was very striking to me. How one does desire our gracious God may give them, and those now baptised, that new name which He has promised.'

Early in November Anna and David decided that a short break in Lagos would be desirable as they were both feeling worn out and in need of recuperation to refuel their energy. On 17th November Anna's journal tells: 'I am now writing in the room where, nearly three years ago, I had my first African fever. It is wonderful to sit here, and think on the way in which we have been led; many and great have been the sorrows, trials and afflictions; but how great, how rich the love and mercy of our God and Saviour: everything must be swallowed up in the remembrance that truly goodness and mercy have followed me all the days of my life.'

'November 26th: The mail arrived with a most delightful packet of letters. Though fortunate and favoured every mail, I never had such a goodly heap, forty-one letters, or notes and such boxes and parcels of things for ourselves, the children, and people. How very kind are friends, known and unknown, in dear England. It is very pleasant and refreshing to us to be so kindly remembered and cared for by many, rich and poor, enabling us to give so much pleasure, not only to the little ones, but to chiefs and others, to whom it is necessary to make presents; and these nice things from their white friends' country produce a very kind and friendly feeling in the poor African's heart, and they often say, what good kind people they must be in that far country. I wish the kind givers could see the happy faces and sparkling eyes, when their things are displayed. But by this mail came another rich present for Africa, two new missionaries, Mr. Buhler and Mr. Hoch. They appear so fresh, and full of spirit and energy, quite refreshing to us to see, who have been melting away, as it were, in the past three years.'

The Revd. Gottlieb Frederick Buhler was a very talented German scholar and was on his way to the Mission at Abeokuta. Mr. James Jonathan Hoch was to replace Mr. Kefer.

'Ibadan, December 15th: We reached our dear home again, with our friend Mr. Hoch, brought safely through the bush by the good hand of God upon us. We arrived amidst warm greetings and welcomes from many, surprising others greatly by the sight of another white man, when they had been doing their best to get rid of us by their persecution of our young converts. The fire and fury of persecution has raged to a very great extent; our hearts have ached, and still ache, for the sufferings of the little flock. Satan fights because his kingdom is endangered. The country priests fight under their master's banner, because their cruel lies and deceit are being exposed. The second Psalm just describes our state: The heathen rage; the people imagine a vain thing; kings set themselves; the rulers take counsel together against the Lord. Their power of endurance is wonderful. There is, no doubt, something of this in the natural character of the Africans; but that there is something much deeper is quite evident; even their persecutors ask, "What is it?" and they think we have some charm in our eye, and they are therefore trying to keep some of them quite out of our sight.'

Anna at this point relates the stories of several of their converts who were cruelly and lengthily persecuted for attending the church services or even having anything to do with the Mission house.

'The story of one young woman is most touching and interesting. She stands with the courage of a dependant child on the love, mercy, and help of a great and gracious God. Her marriage was hastened by her parents, who thought it would prevent her coming to church. Her husband treated her even more cruelly than her parents, which had been hard enough. When told by him, "You shall never enter white man's house again", she said, "Very well; as you wish it, it shall be." "Neither shall you go to his church." To this she replied, "I can not and will not submit; it is God's house; I will go." She was then cruelly beaten with sticks and cutlasses, and stoned, till her body was swelled all over; a rope was tied round her neck, and she was dragged, as an ox to the slaughter, to her father's house. Mr. Hinderer went to beg them to cease their cruelties. He found her lying prostrate before the idols, which had been brought out for her to worship: she was held there by furious people, who were shouting "Now she bows down! Now she bows down!" She exclaimed, "No, I do not! It is you who have put me here; I can never bow down to gods of wood and stone, which cannot hear me. Only in Jesus Christ, the Son of God, the only Saviour of poor sinners, can I trust." She was then, dragged up; they took a rope to put round her throat, saying, "Well, we will take you away, and kill you!" She replied, "Kill me if you will, the sooner I shall be with my Saviour in heaven; but I will not, I cannot, serve these foolish things."

They did not kill her; but for months she endured every kind of ill-treatment, and at last ran away to Abeokuta. The history of her journey is little short of a miracle, and reminded me of the angel opening the door for Peter. One of her companions in suffering had run away before; she told me she felt she could stand it no longer; she was weak in body and mind, and she feared they would lead her back to heathenism, so she would go away the first opportunity. She is the seventh child who has run away from her father's house; the former six went on account of the tyranny and cruelty of the father; but now they rally round him, and help him with cowries to make charms, and to bribe the chiefs to be angry with us and say, "What a bad girl this is to go away, and what a bad thing this church matter is."

Another young woman has been set free. Her intended husband refused to have her, and made her parents pay back what he had given for her, which they gladly did for fear lest she should run away. So she comes to church, and lives at home as usual.

A young girl of sixteen years has been nearly killed by her father for coming to church; beaten with a cutlass till she could not feed herself, or turn on her mat. She has endured very much, but I fear she is giving way now; she does not come to church. On a week-day she visited me; I reminded her of the words of our Saviour, which she had learned with me, "Whosoever shall confess Me before men, him shall the Son of man also confess before the angels of God; but he that denieth Me before men, shall be denied before the angels of God." She wept, poor child, but alas! I saw her last Sunday go to fetch water from the brook, which, with every other kind of work, she had stoutly refused hitherto, even when they would not let her leave the house. She has told them for nearly twelve months, "This is God's day!" Will you not pray for her, and for these young beginners in the ways of the Lord, that they may be kept, helped, and strengthened?

Another has equally and patiently suffered the whip, the rope, and the chain, has been dragged about from one town to another, to make her forget about coming to church and serving God but she was too much in earnest to forget by being carried to a far country. After some weeks of absence, she was brought back; her father promised her great things, clothes, beads, honour, and added, "Now you will never go there?" pointing to the church. "Father, she replied, I am just the same as before, I will be a good daughter to you, I will earn cowries for you, only let me go to God's house, to hear His word and follow it, for this I cannot give up." The father said, "What strength do these white people give! What charm have they! Nothing will make these people give up!" and he nearly yielded. "It is of no use," he said, "I am tired." But his neighbours came about him, and gave him no rest till he promised to prevent his daughter coming to us.

The mother had come and said that if we would persuade her to worship idols as well, she might come to church. The girl has since often been sent to Ijaye to buy things; she was to go on Saturday, and come back on Monday; but then they found she could go to God's house there, so that was given up ; and one Sunday she was called out of church, but did not go. On the following Sunday, hearing her mother getting the chain ready to tie her, she ran to us, and what a fearful noise we heard! The whole family came into our yard, and flourished about their swords and knives, which we knew they would not use: we left them till they were tired, and then they went away. The girl was then advised to go home and sit down quietly for that day, which she did; and, though the house is close to us, we heard no more noise. She visited me secretly a few evenings since, and told me her heart was in the same place, and that she would follow the way God had sent us to teach, unto death. They have told her they will carry her to those who sell slaves, and who send them far away; her answer was, "Well, where you send me, I will go. God, the great God, my God, is in all the world." You will readily believe how keenly we partake with them in their sufferings; though we weep, yet do we rejoice that they are so wonderfully supported; and we thank God that He has permitted His children to make such a good confession of their faith before so many.

The father of one of these young women has this morning set her free to go to God's house, and to walk in the way she sees right; for he says, "It is true what that white man says, it is no use to fight against God."

Another man is greatly troubled at what he has done, and is quite in an agony to see his child once more.

The mother of a third now begs me to help her to find her child. Her heart yearns after her whom she so fearfully persecuted, under evil direction. In other houses the cry is, about those who escaped, "Oh, if it had not been for you, this would not have happened." So our God has graciously made His arm to be felt among us, and many hear Him say, "Why persecutest thou Me? It is hard for thee to kick against the pricks." The Lord will not forsake His own work; when it pleaseth Him, He can put all His enemies to silence.

Even these poor deluded heathens tell us, "Have patience, white man; your words and ways are new, we are dark and have no sense, tell your word day after day, it will go into the ear, and bye and bye many will follow it."

Several of the young women described in the preceding extracts, and who were at this time so bold and courageous in confessing Christ, brought dishonour afterwards on their profession, and grieved the hearts of those who were now rejoicing in their first zeal and love for Christ and His Gospel; but there is reason to hope that at least two of them were afterwards brought to a better mind and now seek to glorify God, and lead a consistent Christian life.'

## 1856

By the dawn of 1856 life at the Mission had settled into a pattern of Sunday services and Sunday schools for adults and children and evening hymn singing. The rest of the week was devoted when possible to preaching by the men, day school for the children and household management and visiting for Anna. Anna had overflowing love for all the people she came into contact with. Her joy was increased by writing about them and sharing her amusement and sorrows with the recipients of her letters.

'February 4th: My little African boys and girls are going on well so far, and are sheltered from much evil, but need the rod of correction now and then. The three younger boys must eat a fruit which I told them not to eat, as it was not ripe. They thought it was ripe, or that it would not do them any harm. The consequence was, after a little while, they were crying with smarting and immensely swelled lips. One of the elder boys laughed at them, and told them they would die. They were now quite frightened, and did not know what to do. So, one of them, Akielle, said "What naughty boys we have been! We have been like Adam and Eve, eating the forbidden fruit, let us go and pray to God, and ask Him not to let us die this time, and we will not do so any more" and so they went with all childlike simplicity and prayed, and then came to me to forgive them for not obeying my word. The next morning to their great joy their lips were better. It was a simple affair, but I was glad to feel these little ones knew the meaning of prayer, and I did indeed desire they might always remember the Throne of grace and mercy, in all their future paths, with the same simplicity and confidence.

You must share my sorrows as well as my joys. Another little boy has been taken from me by his heathen parents, a child who has been a long time with me. The worst is, I can never see him, he does not come near me, so that I cannot tell whether his heart is still with us, or whether he has been turned to former fashions. It is a sore trial to me. I have felt I would rather have laid him in our quiet burial ground. Oh how many drops of bitterness there are in the missionary's cup! but the great and glorious Ruler of heaven and earth can bring good out of evil.'

'March 2nd: It is raining tremendously; we have had a fearful tornado, both last evening and this. It is such an enjoyment to be able to shut up our house now all round, it is quite a luxury in these tornadoes, and we only wonder how we lived with out this necessary comfort.'

'May: It is fearful to see the poor heathens intense love of life, they will do anything, spend any thing and everything, to be assured by priests and orishas that they shall live long; and their principal salutation, by way of desiring a special blessing is "Olurun bunolemi - God grant you long life!" and no wonder, for what is their hope beyond the grave? It is so very dark to them; they never like to talk about it. But from what one can gather, it seems to them something so completely unknown, they have no idea what is to follow death. They have I think a belief in the transmigration of spirits, by the fact that there is one kind of animal which the bush-hunter never kills, because he thinks it is one into which the spirits of hunters will go after death. Others are supposed to inhabit palm-trees. This is I think confirmed by the practice of consulting the orisha at the birth of a child, with a view to ascertaining which of his ancestors now inhabits that child, and when it is decided, the 'country fashion' of that ancestor must be followed by the child. Then there is the custom of the spirits appearing, called egungun, the bone people; the ancestors are supposed to be called from the other world, to come and speak with their relatives.

They are not to be seen in the grove, but their voices are to be heard; and to gain this, yams, fowls, sheep, goats, and cowries must be brought, which of course become the property of the country priests, whose hands are full through these delusions. There is an egungun grove not far from us, and the yells and groans and miserable sounds are terrible. I have felt it sometimes as most awful in the solemn stillness of the night, while watching my poor husband or others in illness.

There are bad spirits too, who are supposed to cause most of the evils of life, and those who have reason to fear them wear rattling clinking irons round their ankles, which are heard at every movement of the foot, and the noise is supposed to frighten the spirits away. When a pair of these jingling feet walk in, during our Sunday services, it gives one a thrill of horror, it is so demon-like. These poor people year after year, day after day are seeking for relief from the greatest burden of the heart, but, are so slow to believe the word of Jesus, "I will give unto you eternal life;" so deaf to the exhortation, "Come unto Me that ye may have life; without money and without price." Oh that the Spirit of God would descend and enlighten these dark souls, and breathe upon these dead bones! Then would this wilderness rejoice and blossom as the rose.

I think no preacher or teacher of the gospel can feel so entirely his own weakness and helplessness, the entire dependence he must rest on the Spirit and blessing of God, as the missionary amongst the heathen. It is not the planter or waterer, but God alone, who must do His own work; but as He chooseth to use means, He commits the outward work to earthen vessels, in His inscrutable wisdom. May we in the day of toil, in the ploughing and sowing, labour cheerfully and with a rejoicing hopeful spirit, leaning on the strong arm; and if the reaping and ingathering day into the church militant be given us here below, may we give the honour and glory where alone it is due, as we surely shall if the fruit of the seed sown now is not seen till we have become inhabitants of the better land.

We are now in the midst of the rainy season, and very cooling and refreshing it is. A few days since, I went with the children to the rice farm. A shower came on, but we had set our minds upon it, therefore I would not mind pushing through the wet grass; but there was a brook to cross, and "What will Iya do now?" was the cry. There was a large stone on which the people wash clothes; this stone was placed in the middle of the brook, and by it I could step nicely across. There was a little boy there, a stranger to us, watching the whole affair, who seemed to think it very extraordinary I could not walk through the water like other people. Now their little black skins are as full of roguery and mischief as any little boy at home, so in our absence he prepared an adventure for our return. There lay the stone, but underneath, the little urchin had placed a smaller and uneven one, so when I stepped on it, over it goes, and plump go my feet into the water, and then he comes forward with his salutation of sympathy "Pele, pele, pele o - Softly, take care, don t hurt yourself." We should not call this very civil, but I could not help thoroughly enjoying the bit of fun for the little rogue.'

In her journal on May 6th, Anna told a most heart-rending story: 'In 1854, a war broke out between Ibadan and Efon. Until that time Ogunyomi was a happy child at home, living in peace with her father, mother, and two brothers, in the town of Efon. When the war began, all the able-bodied men were compelled to join the army, and amongst them was Ogunyomi's father. He was never heard of again, and most probably had fallen in battle. His town was destroyed, the men and youths were killed; and the women and children, after wandering about in despair and misery, were taken prisoners, and sold for slaves. A few, stronger than the rest, contrived to escape into the bush, and amongst them were Ogunyomi and her mother. Fear drove them farther and farther. Their only food was roots and leaves. When they had threaded their way for two or three days, through the dark and pathless thicket, they began to hope that they were safe from their enemies. But they were afraid to speak above a whisper, lest they should be heard and overtaken. Exhausted with hunger and fatigue, they at last lay down to rest, under the shelter of a great tree. At once two men sprang suddenly upon them. One seized the mother, and the other the child. Their tears and entreaties were useless. They were torn from each other, and hurried off in different directions. The little girl, who was only seven years old, was taken to Ibadan, and put up for sale in the market. A Christian man, who himself had once been a slave, touched by her sorrowful face, took her in his arms, and tried to comfort her. Hearing that she was soon to be taken down to the coast and stowed away in a slave ship, he longed to purchase her and set her free; but it was beyond his power. He therefore went to the mission-house, told her sad story to Mr. and Mrs. Hinderer, and entreated them to redeem her. They gladly gave him money for her ransom, and in a few minutes the kind-hearted man brought the little girl to her new home.

The poor child had never before seen a white face, and she screamed with terror when she found herself in the presence of the missionaries. The other children in the compound gathered round her, and told her how happy they were, and that all who lived in the mission-house were safe from slavery. She soon learned, herself, to love her white mother and was constantly found at her side. When strangers came to the house, she clung closely to her, fearing lest they should carry her away. But her great delight was to sit on the floor near to Mrs. Hinderer, and puzzle over the alphabet, or the still greater mysteries of needle and thread. Singing was a pleasure to her, and she quickly learned simple prayers and easy texts. She was a child of a happy disposition, and often her hearty laugh rang through the compound. But a change came over her. Her laugh was heard no more, and her countenance was sad and troubled. Mrs. Hinderer asked, "What is the matter, Ogunyomi? Is any one unkind to you?" "Oh, no," she said quickly. "Then what makes you sad?" She burst into tears, and sobbed out, "Iya mi, iya mi! - My mother, my mother." Mrs. Hinderer tried to comfort her, and promised to have a diligent search made for her mother. But, in a large town of more than a hundred thousand people, this was no easy task, especially as slaves usually received a new name; besides which, it was not known whether the poor woman was in Ibadan, or had been carried away to some other place. Meanwhile she said to Ogunyomi, "You have learned to pray to God, He loves to receive the prayers of little children. Pray to Him, if it be His will, to restore your mother to you." From that time forward, to all her prayers she added the simple petition, "God, give me back my mother." Ogunyomi gradually became happier, but there was still an expression of sorrow upon her face, stamped there by her longing after her lost mother.

When she had lived about six months in the mission-house, she went one morning, as usual, with the other little girls, to draw water from the neighbouring brook. The children were laughing and playing together, when a woman passed by, and, being attracted by the unusual sight of their white clothes, she stood still for a moment, and watched them as they played. One voice appeared to be familiar to her. She raised the basket from her head, placed it on the ground, and listened attentively. Yes, it was her child's voice! Trembling in every limb, she cried out, "Ogunyomi!" Ogunyomi turned round, stared for a long time at the woman, and then, with the cry, "My mother, my mother!" threw herself into her arms. The other children ran to the house, exclaiming, "Ogunyomi has found her mother." It was difficult to believe the joyful news. The poor woman was at first afraid of the white people; but when she heard from Ogunyomi how kind and good they were, and that they had rescued her from slavery, she was at a loss for words wherewith to express her joy and gratitude. She threw herself on the ground and sobbed aloud. When her mind was somewhat more composed, she listened with interest to the story of her child, and then explained that she herself had been sold for a slave in Ibadan, but that happily she had been bought by a kind master. She was obliged to hurry away, but she was comforted by the thought of Ogunyomi's happiness, and rejoiced in the prospect of being able to see her, whenever she might have permission from her master.

Ogunyomi's heart that night overflowed with gratitude to God, who had so graciously heard and answered her prayers. For many weeks all went on well. The mother often came to see her child. Then her visits ceased, without any explanation. Mr. and Mrs. Hinderer were troubled for the child, and, after much enquiry, they discovered that the mother was seriously ill, and that all hope of her recovery was gone. For Ogunyomi's sake they paid the poor woman's ransom, and removed her to the mission-house. For ten months she was nursed and cared for by these new friends, and then, to the joy of all, especially of her own child, she recovered. When her health was sufficiently re-established, she was employed as cook for the children, and found much happiness in the altered circumstances of her life.'

Anna and David received another important invitation which they knew must be accepted. It was to visit the King of Oyo. Oyo city was about 30 miles due north of Ibadan. It was vitally important to build up good relationships with local rulers as without their support no mission could possibly flourish. Anna wrote: 'June. Our visit to Oyo, the king's city, is happily accomplished and now I sit down to tell you about it. On May 28th we started, I travelling partly on horseback and partly in my hammock. It was very, very hot, and not having been out for some time, I soon felt very tired, and was thankful for willing carriers, two of our own people, and two from our young friend's house, the Balogum Olumloyo. ... At last we reached Ijaye, after full seven hours journey, and glad indeed we were to be under the shelter of a mission-house, with Mr. [Adolphus] Mann. [This CMS mission was founded at about the same time as theirs at Ibadan.] We intended to start for Oyo next day, but Mr. Mann's invitation to stay and rest a day was too tempting, so on the third day we left for Oyo. The road lay through grass fields, but it was such a nice sandy road that I enjoyed riding nearly all the way, and it was rather a cloudy day too, which is such a luxury in this country. In six hours we reached the king's city, and Mr. Hinderer was received by the people as an old friend.

Our Daniel Olubi had been there several weeks. Mr. Hinderer had placed him there to commence teaching till the appointed person came up. He was very glad to see us, and so were all the people of the compound. A nice little place the king had given Mr. Hinderer, for any one to reside in till a proper house was built. This had all been repaired and made comfortable, by the king's orders, so that we had quite a home to go to; a great deal larger than the native house here, in which we lived more than a year. We had hardly changed our clothes, and begun to refresh ourselves, before the king's messenger came to say we must go to the palace; and, before he had done speaking, came another and another, saying the king was in haste to see us. A good deal of this was court etiquette. So we made haste, and were received in great state, but the king's face was quite uncovered; and he received Mr. Hinderer with great joy, saying he was his friend, his beloved friend, and had not forgotten that his name was Dabidi (David).

He praised him for bringing his wife, and then asked if he might salute me; then he asked me of my welfare, how I had left Ibadan, and if I had heard lately from my own country of my father and mother, brothers and sisters (for in Africa every one who comes from your town is your brother or sister), and was the good Queen of England well? I answered that all was peace. "Alafia ombe mbe;" he was pleased, and said his heart rejoiced to see us, and then with true gentlemanly thought and politeness, he said he would not keep us longer, as we must be tired from our journey: we must go and eat and rest, and to-morrow see him. On Sunday we had nice services in the piazza, though I was obliged to be on my stretcher in a corner, having fever, but I rejoiced to see quite a goodly gathering of regular attendants, whom our Olubi had drawn together.

There were many others besides. My husband read several of our church prayers and the litany, that beautiful litany which draws such a hearty response in every language; and then he spoke to them on the forgiveness of sins. In the afternoon we had the same gathering, and so passed the day. Before leaving Oyo, Mr. Hinderer had a conversation with the king and described to him the purpose of his visit, to which he listened attentively, and then turning to his people, said, "The white man is my beloved friend, he shall teach God's word, and preach it in my town; what do you say?" They answered, "It is good we receive white man with all our hearts."'

Anna and David were treated as most honoured guests during their stay there and came away with very thankful hearts that they had had such a good reception. They prayed that many blessings would follow when the gospel had been heard there.

One young girl named Konigbagbe was so captivated by Anna that she wished to go with her to Ibadan. Her mother agreed with little reluctance that she could go and was more concerned that first permission had to be obtained from the King as she lived in one of his houses. Anna was pleased to take care of her and so she went to live with them at the Mission and when she was a little older became Anna's very devoted personal maid.

On the journey back they stayed only one night at Ijaye 'and started the next morning early for Ibadan, and found all well, and a joyful welcome. On Sunday we were surprised and rejoiced to see a large attendance at the church, of men and women. The agreement the persecutors made to prevent any one coming, is now broken, and the road is once more free again.'

Soon after this Anna had to report that 'We were just rejoicing and girding up our loins with fresh zeal and vigour for our work, when my dear husband is laid very low with yellow fever, just what poor Mr. Kefer died of. He has not been well the last six months, not three weeks without fever. For ten or twelve days he is well, and goes out preaching, and then is sick again. After all this, 1 did not think he would have a severe illness, but it has come, and he is now as weak as a baby.

It has pleased God once more to spare his life, yet seeing how he is, and the danger of another attack, we all feel it is a real duty that he should go at once to England for health's sake, so that

I am now nursing him, and packing, and preparing to leave poor Ibadan by the mail which will leave the end of next month, July; so a month after you receive this, you may expect to see us, if it please God to give us a safe and prosperous voyage. I am sure you will feel for us in the real sorrow and trial it is to have to go so suddenly. It is such a sorrow and such a wrench, which even the joy of seeing our beloved friends again cannot mitigate. I cannot write more; it is well I shall have hard work these next few weeks.'

And then there was a truly delightful surprise: 'June 19th: It has come out to-day that Olubi and Susanna have fallen in love with each other, and wish to be married before we leave. So here is another iron in the fire, but one that gives us real satisfaction. I must now prepare for the bride's outfit.'

The wedding must have been a wonderful opportunity for rejoicing by everyone connected with the Mission. Susanna and Olubi had both been very close to Anna and David during their time at there. Susanna in addition to being Anna's personal maid was also greatly involved in the management of the household. Olubi was already proving himself to be a wonderful teacher and his wisdom and communication skills over many issues were proving to be invaluable.

So, Anna and David's first stay at the Ibadan Mission ended with a very happy occasion. The second stay would sadly not end in the same way.

# Chapter 5 The first home leave 1856 to Autumn 1857

Arrangements had to be made for the oversight of the Mission during David's absence. The Revd. James Hoch was already there as his assistant and it was agreed that the Revd. Gottlieb Buhler, with whom he had travelled to Africa, should come from Abeokuta to work alongside him. It seems that Ibadan was regarded as an outpost of the Abeokuta Mission.

Remembering how the children had reacted on previous occasions when Anna had to leave the Mission, she knew that the days of preparation for leaving for England and the day of departure were going to be extremely difficult. Anna wrote in her journal: 'I must pass over all those trying preparations; they were very sorrowful. My children, I shall never forget your weeping, and how you held me to keep me back, so that grown up people wept at the sight.

We reached Lagos in July, to be ready for the mail, and had a miserable time there; but on the 1st of August we went on board the steamer, homeward bound, though I think I then felt that I was rather leaving home. I was ill from the day we left Lagos till the very day we reached Plymouth. When the captain kindly helped me up the steps on landing, he said, "Thank God, Mrs. Hinderer, that I land you in England! I never expected this, but always had the misery of thinking that we should bury you in the deep sea."'

The steamer that sailed from Lagos on the 2nd August 1856 was the *S.S. Retriever*, carrying mail, passengers and cargo. It was Captain M'Intosh who bade farewell to Anna and David when they disembarked at Plymouth on 4th September with the other 14 passengers on board.

'On a Saturday evening we arrived in London, and lodged near the Church Missionary House. We much enjoyed our peaceful Sabbath, though feeling the cold. Can you understand my relief to have my dear husband under medical care and skill after all we have gone through? He has had much suffering, and certainly was never really well the last year and a half; but I do trust in a short time he will be in a very different state. I am thankful to feel very fairly well. A little tired sometimes; and I find I am not the strong person I was before I went to poor Africa.'

Once David was recovering they went to Lowestoft to stay and then Anna was suddenly painfully ill. The nature of the illness is not known. However, she was greatly cheered by the concern and sympathy of her many old friends. But there was one friend who was no longer there that she missed tremendously. That of course was Mrs. Cunningham. When she was fit enough, Anna, still feeling very weepy, went to sit by her grave in St. Margaret's churchyard to pray. From Anna's description in a letter it is apparent that Richenda Cunningham was an extremely wise woman.

The tomb of Richenda and Francis Cunningham in Lowestoft Churchyard

'We may look far and wide for her equal. I do not know what shone most brightly in her; everything appeared in its full beauty and force. Her extraordinary powers, with her sweet humility, and every Christian grace; her meekness, gentleness, forbearance, that loving charity, which can hardly be equalled; I never saw such pure generosity. I think I knew more of her gifts and helps while living with her than almost anyone. Writing for her, and waiting upon her as I did, I could not help knowing her; and besides, she would speak to me about things and people in many a quiet hour over her drawing. Never did I see, nor can I expect to see again, such an exemplification of that charity which thinketh no evil; always so willing and ready, and I may add determined, to look on the best side. In this evil world it was impossible such a kind heart should not be encroached or imposed upon. When talking one day of a person who did not seem worthy of her kindness, she only tried to speak of what might be good and hopeful. I remember asking her if she did ever see any evil or wrong in anybody. She looked up from her drawing, a little amused, and smiling said, "Why yes, dear, I see it, but I like to shut one eye, and open the other only a very little way, when there is anything wrong; and besides, I like honey so much better than poison, that I like to seek only after the honey." It is indeed a wonderful privilege, and how great a responsibility, to have been under the influence of such a spirit, and such a daily and hourly example!'

Sadly Anna's father was not there to greet her either. Her journal tells that 'Just before starting for England, I heard of my dear father's rather sudden but peaceful and happy death. I cannot mourn for him, for I believe him to be one whom his Saviour loved, but one deeply tried and afflicted in this world; he now rests in Jesus; from the burden of the flesh and from grief and fear released.' Although Anna had left home in her teenage years she had always kept in close touch with him and the family.

It was probably during their stay in Lowestoft that Anna and David first met the Reverend William Nottidge Ripley who was an assistant Curate at Lowestoft at that time. He was to prove a very good friend to them in later years.

## 1857

At the beginning of 1857 they stayed with friends in London for a while. David was in demand as speaker at public missionary meetings. Anna spoke at more informal gatherings and private functions. These meetings were extremely important for raising people's awareness of their work and encouraging them to give financially to support the work of CMS. But Anna was not well and was regularly in touch with her doctor - Dr. Johnson - but seems to have almost accepted that feeling unwell was normal for her in view of the severe illnesses suffered in recent years.

In April of that year they went to Halesowen to stay with the family of the Reverend Richard Hone, whose daughters compiled the first book about Anna – 'Seventeen Years In The Yoruba Country'. A member of his family had read of David's work in the magazine *Church Missionary Intelligencer* and had corresponded with Anna and David during their time at Ibadan and sent clothes for the children, so they knew each other well on paper but not in person. During the three weeks they spent together they built up a very strong relationship resulting in the exchange of correspondence in later years which became increasingly welcome to Anna and David.

From Halesowen they travelled to Yorkshire before returning again to London. This visit was to enable Anna to seek further medical advice from Dr. Johnson. This time he advised that mineral baths might be helpful. They had been intending to go to Germany to visit David's friends and relatives, so their plans for that were brought forward. This would be a real holiday. They left on June 5th and took a trip on the River Rhine followed by the train to Basle. They went on to the Bernese Oberland to enjoy the magnificent alpine scenery before going to Wurtemburg to take the waters at Berg and stay with David's relatives in the

Schorndorf neighbourhood. It was a time for them to relax completely and recuperate.

They also met many of the people whom David knew well and were strong supporters of the work in Africa. Anna wrote: 'The sincere and earnest piety of these simple Christians is very beautiful. One poor woman said to me: "For five years and sixteen days I have not failed to pray for you and your husband every day." Just five years ago D was in this country, and told them about Africa, and that we were going soon together; and from that time the good woman had borne us on her heart before God. Oh, what a comfort it is to know their prayers are heard by our Father in heaven! Oh, how blessed it is to labour for Him, and, for the little we give up, so abundantly does He reward!'

Anna and David were kept informed about the happenings at the Mission in letters from Daniel Olubi who described what took place at one of the special non-Christian feast days. 'You will be glad to hear Akielle begins to show light to his parents. A few days ago his father sent for him; the boy went, and found all his family engaged making yearly sacrifice; sheep were slain, and the blood sprinkled about, a number of the people rubbing their foreheads in the dust, and the orishas of the family all brought out. The little boy thought to himself he had better go back, but the father, seeing him, called him near and said, "Now, Akielle, I want you to worship with us; here is Erinle (pointing to one of the idols), here is the god who gave you to me." The child, quite in African character, replied by asking some witty question, "If Erinle gave me to you, father, how many children has he left for himself?" The father was puzzled, and said, "Perhaps none". "Well, then," said the boy, "I don't think he would have been so foolish as to give me to you, if he had none left to himself." Then the father said, "Well, you must worship with us." The boy answered, "No, father, I cannot." "Why can't you?" "Why, father, because the Word of God says, "Thou shalt have none other gods but me." As they remained quiet, the child went on and repeated the second Commandment. He was then asked several questions, which he answered readily and respectfully, when the father ended by saying, "Well, Akielle, there is one thing you shall do." The little fellow now thought, my father is going to flog me, or make me worship these things; but the end of the sentence was, "You shall go back to the mission-house, where you have been taught." So he came back with great pleasure.'

Back in England in September the call of Africa became increasingly strong and preparations were made for their return. Anna wrote: 'We rejoice to go to our work, and to our dear people in Ibadan; their earnest desire for us is very pleasing. We had cheering accounts on the whole, last mail. The few disciples are drawing others to hear the blessed words of the Gospel; but another thing touches our hearts. Our good friend Olumloyo [a local chief and father of Akielle] is killed in battle; we have shed tears for him. Alas, alas, he heard the Gospel, and acknowledged its sweetness and its truth, but could not follow it.'

Having completed all the preparations Anna and David set sail for Africa from Plymouth on Saturday 24th October. This time the voyage was on the *S.S.Candace*, a fine new iron-hulled ship owned by the African Steamship Company of Liverpool. Seventeen days later they landed at Sierra Leone where they planned to spend time to see the very beautiful countryside inland and visit other missionaries. This included going to Charlotte to see the school run by Mrs. Sabina Clemens – a widow who had stayed in Sierra Leone after the death of her missionary husband. The school was a much admired pioneering girls' school – the Liberated African Institution - financed by the Church Missionary Society. Was this the inspiration for a future school in Ibadan?

Of a journey into the mountains Anna wrote; 'We passed through Regent, the place itself is a picture. I cannot describe it; it is equal to some parts of Switzerland, and that is saying much. There was no missionary there then, but we went to the empty mission-house, and there we found an old man, with his woolly hair quite white. It seems he lived there all alone, to take care of the empty house. I asked him if he remembered Mr. Johnson, [a missionary] and I touched a chord in the old man's heart. "Ah, me know Massa Johnson, me know him; I been live with him all the time he live here." I wish I could give you the whole account, but we talked together for an hour and a half; and the old man took us into the garden, and showed us a very large orange tree. He gave me plenty of fruit, and said, "Eat these oranges, and take the seeds, and plant them in the Yoruba country, and call it Massa Johnson's orange tree. Massa Johnson plant this tree, I stand by him, and you now, a stranger, eat the fruit" and the dear old man never tired of talking of Massa Johnson, and we talked of heaven, the home of the blessed and faithful missionary. This was a delightful visit. I am only sorry I cannot do justice to it with my pen.'

Massa Johnson was probably the Revd. William Augustin Bernard Johnson who was a missionary to Sierra Leone from about 1816. He died in 1823. Sometime later Anna mentioned an orange tree growing at Kudeti. Was it grown from a seedling of Massa Johnson's tree?

Another place they visited was the village of Hastings. David was 'head-hunting'! He needed to find other helpers for the Mission at Ibadan and wished to recruit Yoruba-speaking people. A great many people from the Yoruba country who had been taken into slavery and later liberated to live in Sierra Leone were glad of an opportunity to be repatriated. There he found Henry Johnson (no connection with the Johnson previously mentioned), a former slave originally from the Yoruba country. He had had a very good Christian education, was a keen supporter of his local church and was enthusiastic for the spread of the gospel. He also found William Allen, a young African schoolmaster born in Sierra Leone, who was equally enthusiastic. They were both willing to move – Henry Johnson with his family of a wife and six children – to Ibadan and they accompanied David and Anna on their journey back to the Mission.

Before leaving Sierra Leone Anna, perhaps yearning to be home, wrote: 'I long to be in Yoruba again, yet I am glad to have stayed here. I am very well, but my poor husband had a sharp attack of fever for one night and day; not the acclimatizing fever, we do not expect to have that here, but soon enough when we get further up. Oh, may we be preserved to labour on…'

# Chapter 6 The second period of service in Africa

## 1858

It was early January 1858 when Anna and David eventually left Lagos for Ibadan, this time by the overland route of about 80 miles, taking three or four days through the territory of the Ijebu tribe. This route may have been chosen as they had a huge amount to carry and this was the more direct route. The contents of this incredible load were not revealed at the time but did become apparent as time went on. Although it was a well used track, it was so narrow that in many places it was single file for those on foot but nearly impassable for horse riders. It was also an undulating route through very varied countryside of dense bush, forest of gigantic trees, tall grassland, exotic plants and gorgeous butterflies and it was well shaded from the nearly overhead tropical sun.

JOURNEY FROM LAGOS.

The first days after their arrival were extremely busy and it was not until January 27th 1858 that the first letter was written. 'We are too busy settling in this dear place to write much by this mail. Thank God, we are in excellent health, after having suffered a good deal in Sierra Leone and Lagos. We stayed at Lagos till we could send up and have people from the interior to fetch us and our loads, and then was it not a treat to see Ibadan faces once more? We had a delightful journey through the bush, the people so pleased to be taking us back again, and when we halted for the night, with our tent pitched and three or four fires about, and all resting after our day's journey, it was so nice to talk for an hour or more, and hear all about Ibadan doings in our absence; and on the fourth day, when we were within sight of the town, we were all at once startled by such a shout as that bush has hardly heard before. Our children and people had come out to meet us, and just caught sight of us. Oh, it was such a happy meeting! Besides our own people there were many of our heathen neighbours and friends, whose welcome was most hearty, the horsemen galloped and danced backwards and forwards and guns were fired, so that altogether we were nearly deafened. I was in a hammock, and my carriers had hard work to get on, and my husband was nearly pulled off his horse. As we went on, the numbers increased, till we were brought to our own door, on Saturday, January 9.

It was delightful to be in our old house again, everything was made so neat and clean, and a nice meal prepared for us. But all this joy had its sorrow; we missed our friend, Olumloyo [the chief who had been killed in battle] and the people also talked of him, saying how pleased he would have been to have met us, and how far he accompanied us on the road when we went away, and could not bear to part with us, and then tears glistened in many an eye, for he was much respected; but tears could not last long that day. For three weeks or more we had visitors constantly, and such kind presents. We have still quite a farm yard from them. I wish you could see our beautiful ducks, with their green and gold feathers sparkling in the sun, quantities of chickens, goats, and three sheep. Besides these we had corn and yams given us. The chiefs and people seem as though they could not give us welcome enough, and say they were afraid we should not come again, as we had so many troubles from the persecution; but now they love us more than ever.

Far better than all, many people are coming regularly to church, and are anxious to be taught the Word of God. Some have been attending a few months and are now bringing their idols to us, saying, "These things cannot save us, we want to follow Jesus," and then desire that their names may be put down as candidates for baptism.

We have now a large basketful of idols, and last evening a man who had been a large dealer in slaves, brought the irons with which he used to chain the poor creatures, saying, that having been made free by the blood of Jesus, he never should want such cruel things again.

We very soon went to pay our respects to the four chiefs of the town; they had sent some of their servants on the road to help us. They were so pleased to see us. Some time ago these same chiefs were afraid to touch our hands, lest we should convey poison to them; or that our eyes should meet, lest they die. Their cruel country priests and Mohammedan Alufas had told them that these things would surely happen if we were allowed to go near to them. But now, in the face of their deceivers, they took our hands, and expressed their joy in every way, and the head chief would make me sit on his own mat, quite close to him. But I am sorry to tell you that chief is now very ill, and, wonderful to say, Mr. Hinderer is allowed to go and see him. We hope he will be spared, as he is rather better than he was. We sent him a mattress and pillow, and though the chief has a very fine one, Mr. Hinderer saw he needed something more comfortable. The poor man was so pleased and tried to thank him, though he can hardly speak.

The dear children were all well, and so happy to have us back; they have been kindly taken care of in our absence, and we thank God for our helpful catechist and his wife, and our good Olubi. Susanna and Olubi were in full force, very happy, and they have a most charming little boy; his name is Daniel, he is the best tempered child possible, full of fun, and very amusing. Ogunyomi and her mother are extremely happy, and little Arubo, little still. Some of them, we have every reason to believe, are truly converted by the Spirit of God.'

'February 15th: My writing time gets less and less and this terribly hot weather does not help one to push for it. We are thoroughly parched, and must now send far for water. The hot seasons are indeed increasing in intensity, but what a mercy that we are preserved in health, though we look, like everything else, bleached and colourless. My own special flock of twenty-seven children occupy much of my bodily and mental strength, my former ones requiring further instruction, the others a breaking in and training; but it is an encouraging work, and when my strength is gone, some one will be ready to stand in my room. Our Sundays are now quite cheering, such a nice attendance of so many earnest listeners.'

Anna was a tireless worker. Unsurprisingly she easily became exhausted and in May was seriously ill. 'They used often to tell me I was doing too much. For six weeks I could not leave my bedroom. One whole week I knew no one or anything. Many times they gathered round my bed for last moments, but it graciously pleased God to listen to their cry, and to restore me. I do not know what my illness was, but it seems principally caused by my great and constant sufferings at sea; and on coming back, with so much to urge me on, I did a little too much. But I am now quite strong, the cold season came on just when I began to mend, and it has tended greatly to my restoration. We never had it so long or so cold before, but though so good for me, I am sorry to say it does not agree with the natives, and I have still many sick people to attend to.'

'July 26th: I sit down to write again, thank God, in good health. We have been on the eve of civil war, may God preserve us from it! It is only since the Word of God entered this town it has been free from it. My children can tell me dreadful tales of these wars, which before used to happen two or three times a year, when the women and children would run into the farms, or hide in their houses for two or three days. Well may so many of the people say, "Ah white man, you are our friend, you have brought peace into this town"... Our chiefs were never more friendly to us than at the present moment....

Ground [for building] is cheerfully given, and they are desirous to have other [mission] stations. The two men my husband chose in Sierra Leone [Henry Johnson and William Allen] are very satisfactory, and are much liked. They are now having the ground cleared in two places in this town, about four miles apart from each other. We stand in about the middle. In the dry season the building is to begin, and then Johnson will live in one and Allen in the other, so that in less than a year, we trust there will be three bells on a Sunday, calling to the house of God. Several persons from both these quarters come to our church now.'

On August 2nd David set off on another journey of reconnaissance into unknown territory to discover where other mission stations might be planted. Anna always faced these separations with great courage because she had such faith and trust in those left behind at the Mission saying: 'I am just now alone; my dear husband is on his long and important journey eastward. Having been permitted to labour here for seven months, with uninterrupted health, to get things to rights and set other things going, and my health being so thoroughly re-established, he felt quite happy in starting the 2nd of this month. He has been gone nearly three weeks. I do not expect him before four or five more.

I am getting weary to hear from him, it is long now; but as he gets further and further away, it is impossible. One cannot help getting a wee bit anxious, in this land of sickness and death, but he is in good keeping, and it is such a favour to be permitted to commit each other to the gracious care of such a Father, such a Friend. Truly I do not grudge him to his Master's work, and this is one part of it, for which he is peculiarly fitted. Yet I must constantly feel the absence of one so ready to take every burden and lessen every care for me. He carries a happy loving heart and cheerful face and so thoroughly understands these people, and has such tact in dealing with them.

Olubi went with him to the first resting place, and came back next day; he dearly loves his master, and was sorry not to follow him, but he also likes taking care of me in his absence. He and his wife and little boy are very flourishing; the child is quite my pet and plaything, when I have time to play; he is a funny, quick little fellow, and though only fourteen months old, has long run alone, and imitates all I say and do.

My, thirty children are very prosperous, very good, very naughty, and very noisy, just as it happens; then there are lots of people to be cared for and watched over: the sick also fall to my share, and I have had many the last six weeks. I have gone about this town to a greater extent than ever on my good little pony's back. I must do it, our converts cannot go to heathen doctors, where they must make sacrifice, or perhaps be quietly poisoned. But a very amusing part is, some of these doctors come to me now, when they are sick, and get confidential when they have received some good, and bring me bark, leaves, and roots, telling me what they are good for; but with the request I will not make them known, which of course I do not, and I have found some of them very useful.

What do you think Olubi found, when he returned on the 3rd, in this town, in the bush, near a running brook? A little baby not a week old; it had been thrown away by some cruel mother. It was shrieking; no one dared to touch it in this heathen land, but Olubi picked it up, and brought it home, as nice a child as you can see. We know nothing about it, perhaps it was a twin child; the gods do not like twins, so one is often got rid of, and perhaps the poor mother had not the heart to kill her child, and so thought, if the pigs or vultures ate it, the gods would be appeased, and take its spirit to a good place. I always make a point of helping a woman who has twins, if she brings them up carefully, which some do in spite of the idols; but this poor little boy only lived with us three weeks. We did all we could, but it seems he had taken a violent cold, and he must die. I was so sorry D. was not at home to baptize him; we should have named him Moses but I was glad the poor little thing should be cared for, and die, and be buried, instead of the pigs and vultures feasting upon him, though I did wish he might live. We buried him under a shady tree in the bush.'

If he had been baptized, would he have been buried in the little churchyard?

'We have had a great loss here in the death of our native catechist, [James Berber] he was a faithful labourer, and we miss him much. …

We are going on very steadily, and have much to cheer us on our way. It has its rough and thorny places. May God give us grace to thank Him for them, for He knows, though we may not see it, that they also are for our good. We have twenty-nine communicants, thirty-nine candidates for baptism and twelve beside who asked to be taken as candidates for baptism last Saturday. Then we have some baptized who have not come to the Communion yet, and we have several inquirers. Thus the Lord's work is going on, and ought we not to be the more encouraged as it is truly hard ground to work upon?'

'September 23rd: My husband came home from his journey in excellent health, and much cheered and refreshed by his interesting tour. It is wonderful to see him; he has not had a day's illness since we came to Ibadan (in January). I quite feel it is in answer to prayer. We enjoy seeing our little church grow. One of the converts, who lives more than three miles from this station, has been so earnest that he has brought many from his quarter to hear the Word of God; and, thank God, many have not heard in vain. Being so far off, they bring their dinners, and stay here all day; but in the evening those that live anywhere near, before they disperse for the night, meet at his house, and have prayer together. They pray for their minister and teachers, for themselves and for the heathen. Touchingly simple and childlike must their petitions be, when we think that such a little while ago they were all enveloped in heathen darkness. A blessing will come, and does come, from such a state of things as this. Though there are so few to do the work of the Lord, in this immense place, He is graciously doing it Himself in the hearts of His dear children gathered here, and will do much by them, the little seed, the small piece of leaven.'

'October 18th: We had the men of our congregation to a little treat one day this month. We showed them our magic lantern, which delighted and surprised them much; then we gave them sweet tea and biscuits, with a little yam, after which they made nice little speeches, comparing their former state with their present, and spoke of the happiness of believing and trusting in God, and Christ their Saviour, and they thanked me so nicely for the pleasure and information we had given them. Then they talked of their former days of heathenism and how they used to gather round their war captain and after a grand feast prepared for them, they would promise to fight for him, "But," said one, "now you, our dear minister, our friend, our father, and you, our mother, call us so kindly, and shew us such wonderful things, and tell us about them. It is God who has given such sense to people to make such things, that we may get instruction from them and then you have given us such nice refreshment and we are very pleased; but you do not want us to fight and catch slaves for you, so we will now end by asking our minister to put up a prayer for us to the great God, that we may be His children and His faithful servants." All knelt immediately, and with a full heart my dear husband put up a prayer for them and for ourselves, and there was such a beautiful and hearty "Amen" at the end from every heart and lip. Our dear children are progressing in many things, but we have our hopes and fears, our joys and sorrows, there is much of true labour, but a blessed one, a work which brings its reward even in this life.'

On October 20th Anna wrote in a letter, 'God be praised. We are enabled to go on in our work, and with some cheer and joy. We are thankful for our present native helpers. You know a little what Olubi is; and Johnson and Allen, whom we brought from Sierra Leone, are turning out as well. They are truly attached to us, and are so thankful for advice and instruction. They have also learned to read Yoruba, and address the people now very well.'

On November 19th, she wrote of them: 'They are real helpers, satisfied in their calling, liking the place, and attached to us. Johnson is a sterling man … a man well acquainted with his Bible, loving and reverencing it: and he quotes it so readily and appropriately. He is quite his master's right hand, for work among the people and in trying to get up another [mission] station. He is now watching and caring so nicely for the new candidates, and they much respect him. Several of them have chosen him as the witness at their baptism.

Allen is a younger man and very well disposed, and our regard for him increases. He addresses an assembly of people remarkably well, whether in the church or the street, and is becoming much more active. You ask about our singing; it is hearty, but not beautiful. The Africans have not sweet voices, but their enjoyment in it makes up for a good deal.

My dear husband was cheered by his interesting service yesterday (Advent Sunday), nine women and five men gathered round him for baptism, and a most interesting sight it was, trusting as we did they were truly converted persons. They looked so earnest, and had been well instructed; their answers, during the time of preparation, were often quite touching, and in the service, instead of "That is my desire" two or three burst forth with "I will, I will, I will" folding the hands in their earnest way, and again to "Dost thou believe?" "Yes, yes, sir, that only I believe and trust in." All the fourteen were idolaters not long ago. We now have the idols which some of them used to worship; but some worshipped the god of water, others the god of war, and another the god of thunder.'

'November 24th:"I do wish you could see my children, we take real pains with them, and they are in some order, and are getting on very well. They are always about us, and out of school hours I can never stir without a flock round me. God give us grace to labour on for Him, and for the poor heathen around! He has mercifully owned and blessed our labours in this town. We are happy and thankful in our Master's service and only entreat you most earnestly to pray for us, that we may be kept faithful unto the end, and that our heavenly Father may do His own work, notwithstanding the infirmities and sinfulness and helplessness of poor frail man!'

'Christmas Day: We have had a pleasant day altogether, though in the broiling heat it is next to impossible to believe in its being Christmas time. Every one of our people came to-day to church, and all came up to salute us first, and were delighted to receive each a Christmas present of a nice new print bag, to put their books in. My children had a fresh supply of clothes, which made them look so comfortable. We had a nice little service, and, in about an hour after it, all dispersed, and my children sat down to a plentiful supply of food, with all sorts of things in their palaver sauce, which I gave them the pleasure of choosing for themselves yesterday. We then sat down to our own meal, and the children went out to salute some of their friends and relatives, while D. and I had a quiet afternoon, quite to ourselves, and we had such a long talk together as is not often our portion. Since tea we have had a pleasant time with the children, and a nice bright short little service, and plenty of Christmas hymns, and then they went to bed.'

'December 28th: On Friday my dear husband starts for Sierra Leone. Those places he visited eastward wish for teachers, so he proposed to go to Sierra Leone to select Yoruba men from the congregations there, who will make good scripture readers.

Death has entered our dwelling this month, and taken away my youngest little African girl, a little, little sorrowful creature whom we found here on coming back. Her name was Sophy Ajele, she was taken by our catechist, in our absence, because her own mother wanted to sell her; her case had to be taken before the chiefs, and they decided, as the father was willing, that she should be brought up by us. Poor little thing, her early days seem indeed to have been sad ones; for three days at a time her mother would give her no food. Then the parents went away to Ijaye, and I never saw them till the end of last month, when the mother came very quietly, as we afterwards found, to steal the child away; but she found her full of measles. Then she pretended to be so grieved for the dear child, and cursed me for letting her get sick; we had at last to drive her out of the yard, but alas! not before she had given the child something very bad, which produced a. complaint for which no means we could use did any good.

In a few days the mother came again, and we were obliged to have her driven out of the compound; it was quite afflicting to see the dear child clinging to me, and crying: "Oh, do not let my mother take me away, she will only sell me; you are my mother!" and then take my hand and say, "I can go to sleep if you sit by me." The two Sundays she was ill I could not leave her, and thankful was I for health to be with her almost night and day. She was a very silent child, but very obedient, and so attentive to any instruction; I never had to punish her but once, and I shall not forget her sorrow. She was very patient in her illness; during the early part she was so happy, lying or sitting on her mat by my chair, with all the pictures to herself; but when she became too weak for that, she chose out her favourite picture, of Christ blessing little children, and putting it by her side she gave me the others, saying, "Iya, let this always stop here, and when I am better I can look at it." A few days more, and my little Sophy had gone, I humbly believe, where she would see her dear loving Saviour face to face.... I suppose she must have been about eight years old.

My remaining children are well now. I have had five ill. I find these African people and children are very delicate. They have very little constitution.

Our house is very comfortable now, a light grass roof over the iron makes it cooler; all is boarded, no more mats, and we have been painting the whole outside, the boards white and the shutters green, and it really looks so bright and pretty, that people come from far to see what we have done. They seem to wonder what will happen next.

I must tell you, because you kindly pity us more than we deserve. About bread, we have such nice flour this time, and we make delicious bread; this makes up if we should now and then have the barrel low or spoiled.'

## 1859

Although David knew that he would be away on January 1st, he planned that the New Year should start, as was already their tradition, with a service. They already knew the missionary hymn of Isaac Watts. Anna wrote: 'We had a very happy new year's day in Ibadan. We had always intended to carry out the suggestion which came originally from America, that at twelve o'clock in the day, in all parts of the world, that hymn should be sung:

Jesus shall reign where e'er the sun
does his successive journeys run;
his kingdom stretch from shore to shore,
till moons shall wax and wane no more.

People and realms of every tongue
dwell on His love with sweetest song,
and infant voices shall proclaim
their early blessings on His name.

Blessings abound where e'er He reigns:
the prisoner leaps to lose his chains;
the weary find eternal rest,
and all the sons of want are blest.

To Him shall endless prayer be made,
and praises throng to crown His head;
his name like incense shall arise
with every morning sacrifice.

Let every creature rise and bring
peculiar honours to our King;
angels descend with songs again,
and earth repeat the loud Amen.'

Anna does not say which tune they used but it must have been 'Truro' – still a great favourite today.

'As my dear husband was obliged to leave before the new year our people begged that I should have it, and at half-past eleven the room and piazzas were full. I read a few selected passages of scripture, and we had prayer, then entire silence for several minutes, and when the clock struck, we all burst out in that beautiful hymn. We had two or three prayers afterwards, and separated with full hearts. I felt there was much blessing in this little gathering, and the remarks, prayers, and tearful eyes showed that I was not alone in this belief. We have much for which to bless and praise our God at this time in Ibadan. Oh, may He continue it! It was a deeply touching day to me.'

Then Anna suddenly seemed very depressed but like many house-proud people, cheered herself up with some house decorating and planning a trip to Lagos. She wrote: 'I felt I was not to see my dear husband again, and I could not bear the sight of his clothes. But in a day or two I was better, and set about a thorough house-cleaning, and papering the parlour, which I have now accomplished, and have made ready to start on the 20$^{th}$ to Abeokuta for a little visit, and to Lagos, following my good husband's parting advice. Only Konigbagbe and Durojula will be my companions on the journey, with two persons to carry my box, bed, &c. It is rather an adventure, but more pleasant and amusing than not in prospect. Dear Lord, bless my going out and coming in, keep us all under the shadow of Thy wing.'

Surely the wall-paper must have been part of the load which came with them from England. Did Anna also learn to do wall papering in Lowestoft?

Anna and the girls stayed more than a week at Abeokuta where Anna very much enjoyed the company of the friends there before continuing on to Lagos. There she was taken ill but was mercifully nursed carefully by Mr. and Mrs. Maser, the missionaries there. On 27th February the mail steamer anchored off Lagos and to Anna's delight David was one of those who disembarked so it was a happy little party that was able to leave for Ibadan the next day.

As usual they set off by canoe across the lagoon from Lagos, however for some reason their canoe collapsed and disintegrated and they found themselves and all their goods and possessions in the water. Everything was saturated but it must have been fairly shallow water as Anna does not mention anyone being drowned. They had to suffer wet clothes and wet mattresses for the rest of their four day journey to Abeokuta. With Anna still convalescent from her last illness this was very unfortunate. Back at Ibadan she wrote: 'March 16th: With good nursing, medicine, kind friends, and our merciful Father's love, I was restored, and reached Ibadan, through the great kindness of our Christian people, who, on hearing of my sickness, came to carry me in a hammock every step of the way.'

Soon after their home-coming, towards the end of March, the missionaries were delighted to be visited by Bishop John Bowen from Sierra Leone. 'March 28th: How pleasant it is to write from this place again; we are so thankful to be settled once more in our home and our work, having had a most delightful and refreshing few days visit from our dear Bishop. He has left us this morning, and has left a blessing behind him. I wish I could give you a vivid description of him; he is a most delightful man, and well fitted for his work in Africa. Oh, may our God preserve him to us, and to His Church on earth! The Bishop has good health, he has gone through some sharp attacks of fever, and is able to endure much in the way of travelling, and is very free from excitement. … He has been so kind to us, interested in the work, visiting the chiefs, and doing good in every way; ready to listen to our lamentations and rejoicings, so capable of advising or reproving, quick of speech and decided, but with such true Christian courteousness. … On Sunday he confirmed twenty two persons, and gave a most beautiful address, so earnest, faithful, and suitable. …'

'Good Friday 1859: I must write a few lines at the close of this most solemn day. … My dear husband had a service this morning. Every person who comes to church was there. Then he had a prayer-meeting in the afternoon, in which there was much life and heart. Two of the converts and one of the scripture-readers, prayed most earnestly and beautifully; they were evidently not strangers to prayer, they knew what it is to lift up their hearts to God their Saviour.'

Easter Sunday was the great occasion when those who had been confirmed by Bishop Bowen were able to receive their first Communion and fully participate in the joyful service.

Then, followed an event which fully illustrated the importance of the mission to spread the Christian gospel. Anna reported on April 27$^{th}$: 'Our old friend the King of Oyo is dead; there were not so many persons put to death as is usual on such occasions, not more than four men. But forty-two of his wives poisoned themselves, for the honour of accompanying him to the other world.'

Making time for correspondence was always a priority as there were so many people keen for news of the happenings at the Mission. The friends at Lowestoft were always at the forefront of Anna's thoughts. On May 11th, she wrote a special letter to the children of the school at Lowestoft to explain to them the difference between them and the African children. She said: 'Who can wonder at their failings, when we think how they have been brought up? No clothes, no books, nothing to take care of, food easily procured, and in plenty, without trouble or thought to themselves, and with very little to their masters or parents, so that eating is the principal thing with them, and in this they have at home no order, no regularity. They eat whenever they like, sleep when and where they like; so they have plenty to learn when they come to us, and, poor children, I dare say they do not like it much at first.

You would have been rather amused at our washing palavers. I would have them wash every morning, but this was to them an unheard-of absurdity; and it had come to this, that any child who refused must have no breakfast: but if you had seen them you would have thought they were all going to be whipped. However, they have overcome that difficulty now, and are so fond of the regular refreshing wash that they would almost go without their breakfast rather than without their bath. There is plenty of work with and for them, to get a little order, rooms cleared up, clothes right, water fetched and necessary duties performed by them. I get so tired by half-past eight that I often do not want any breakfast, yet I am encouraged, I know these are the very things these children require to be taught.'

When the post arrived on July 26th they heard of the death from fever of Bishop Bowen. Everyone at the Mission was absolutely devastated at this news as his visit had left a great impression on them all. Anna wrote: 'We are true mourners; we could not have a service this afternoon. Our people were so heartily grieved they could not take a service, and dear D. was too utterly broken down. The people had assembled, so Olubi went and told them what we had heard. There was true sorrow, not the loud wailing of the Africans in general, but quiet weeping; and all dispersed to their homes. To-day, every man and woman who comes to church has been to salute and sympathise with us. Some have just got into the house, and instead of a word you hear a sob, and they have turned round and gone home. Others have tried to speak words of comfort, or sat down in silence.'

Anna's letters to Francis Cunningham were never difficult to write as he was like a father to her and she was forever thankful of the part he had played in her life. On July 7th she wrote, ' Our little church goes on steadily and we look on in hope, but not without some fear and trembling; yet we desire to labour on in faith and hope, and with thankfulness; we are in good health, fully occupied, and very happy. I have felt so much lately what a blessing, what a gift, is good spirits and a cheerful heart. If we had not this blessing, I think we must break down sometimes and how constantly do I feel what a blessing, help and preparation your dear vicarage life was to me with you and dear Mrs. Cunningham at the head; and all one saw, and learned, and felt there; the regular occupied life, the kindness and love which reigned there!

Sorrow and care came, but there one saw how it was to be borne, and a cheerful, blessed spirit presided, loving and loved, all under the banner of Jesus: so much happiness existed, because He was the honoured and beloved Head. Well, I ought to be better than I am for all I learned there; but I always feel I owe everything of the earthly blessing to that dear home, my dear mother dying when I was so young, that I was tumbled up and down in the world a good deal. I am sure the blessing of a light and cheerful spirit (you know in what sense I mean it) is not to be told, especially in African life. Dear friend, you have been a blessing to many; but the day shall declare it. Trials, clouds, difficulties, heartaches, are the portion now very often; but bye and bye all, all will be well. Now it is a mingled cup indeed, but what a mercy it is not all sorrow. No! Life is full of blessings, but it is light and shadow, cloud and sunshine, tears in the evening, joy in the morning. But in our home above it will be all joy, all peace, perpetual happiness, because there we shall be in the presence of Jesus, and there shall be no more sin, and we shall be delivered from this body of sin and death. O when we dwell on this, we long to be gone, to stretch our wings, and fly away; but it is blessed to labour and to wait.

The children are going on well: your Francis Lowestoft Akielle grows a fine fellow, very like his poor father, a nice boy, but I call him the head talker and head noise-maker. He begins to write well. Dan Olubi is a nice little fellow, so well behaved; he is with me all day, eats with us, and talks away to his heart's content, but he knows there are times when he must be silent. He is so fond of pictures, and picks out all sorts of things you would think such a child would never see, and shows them to me. He helps me with Yoruba famously; his last acquirement was to find out in your likeness that you are reading a book, and when we were singing today, he shouts out, "Iya, come look, the great gentleman is singing also" and then he clasps his hands in extreme delight. At church he sits with me like a little mouse; but sometimes he whispers, "Has not dear done talking yet?" He is now asleep on my back, country fashion and a very convenient one; by this disposal of him, I am able to have him often when I could not otherwise.'

'October 25$^{th}$: I must tell you a story of one of my little boys finding his mother, or, rather, of his mother finding him. Any one is free to enter our front yard, and to look, and talk, and be spoken to as much as they wish; but to the back yard we do not allow visitors, as it is necessary to keep that part more private. A few mornings ago, a woman came in to sell cooked yams; another woman followed her, wishing to buy a piece for herself, as soon as she should put the large calabash down from her head. The children all began singing, "You must not come here, wait in the other yard, the yams will soon come to you." So she was going away; but, on looking at one of the little boys, she thought by the marks on his face that she knew something of him. She called him by a certain name, but the little boy did not know it. She asked him some questions, and at last she said, "Don't you know me?" He said, "No, I never saw you before". And then she said, bursting into tears, "I am your mother." She had lost all her four children by war, and this little boy was so small when he was taken away that he had quite forgotten his mother, and what his name was.

There was great joy, as you may believe, in which we all shared; and soon the little boy began to recognise that it was his mother. You will like to know what his name was, though you will not understand it, and I must see his mother again before I can quite tell you the meaning. It was Atipui. And now, how came we by this little boy? A few years ago, a man of this town bought him, intending to make him his slave; but the man afterwards came to church, and became a Christian, and though he had several people whom he had bought, he did not like to hold them as slaves any longer. They come to church with him, and one of them is already baptized; they work for him, and live with him, but are quite free. This was very noble of the man; there are very few of the Africans who do such a thing. So he brought to me the little boy, to whom he gave the name of Ope, (Thanks) saying if I would take the little boy to live with me, and bring him up with my others, he should like it. I was very glad to do this, so here he has been these two years, and he has learned to read very nicely, and begins to write, and is a very happy little boy indeed.

The mother is living in the town. The man who had her as a slave had made her his wife and is very kind to her. She will be able to come and see her little boy whenever she likes. When she heard he would never be a slave again, she did not know what to do with herself for joy. And now, who can tell, perhaps that poor woman, through finding her child, may also find a precious Saviour for her soul. Pray for her, that she and her dear boy may hear and believe the blessed Gospel of our Lord and Saviour, Jesus Christ, and that she may be amongst those who bless God for sending white people to this country to teach and preach good tidings.'

In October Anna recorded: 'My dear husband is exceedingly ill with a terrible cough, which has lasted nearly three months; he has also violent fever, such an attack as he has not had for some years, and he suffers agony from boils, a malady to which Europeans are subject in this country, but which he has entirely escaped until this year. It is a real trial to him to be so much laid aside, but he manages to get through a good deal of home work, and to take the services generally. He has been much interested in having persons come to him together, and separately, for special instruction, before joining us at the Lord's Table on Advent Sunday. He is now having his candidates for baptism, and hopes to baptize seventeen or nineteen on Christmas Day. That he should have this work now is very comforting to him, as he is not able to speak five words in the streets.'

Whilst Olubi went on a visit to Abeokuta in November, Anna looked after the school children who were given a holiday. She wrote on Nov. 30th: 'I have tried to make the holidays pleasant to the children, and we used to go out, in the cool mornings or evenings, nice little expeditions. One day nearly forty of us went to a farm, about three miles off, and stayed the whole day, carrying palaver sauce with us, and buying yams in the farm, and cooking them there in true gipsy fashion. They had fine games under beautiful shady trees, scrambling for cowries, blind man's buff, and all sorts of games, Yoruba and English. I cannot play with them as I could at home, but they like having me there. I am so thankful to see more energy and liveliness about them; their play was much more earnest and pleasant, and so I think has their school work been. The people in the farm, slaves and servants, were much amused to see them, and said, "These children do indeed know how to play." It was such a pleasure to see the boys climbing up trees, though they did tear their clothes, and the girls running, dancing, and jumping about in healthful games. The little ones, who could not walk so far, had dinner and play at home another day.'

The work of making home visits to some of their flock was fitted into Anna's routine whenever possible. 'Last Tuesday it was a nice cloudy morning, so after breakfast I went to see four of our Christians who were sick. I had to travel at least four miles about this town to see them, but my little pony and I are capital friends, and when it is not so very hot, I am glad to be out. Visiting our people is not so easy as in Lowestoft, and how different is our power! I am always about in the house and compound, but if I walk outside a little way, my knees bend under me. So it seems with us all; my husband seldom can walk any distance, so our ponies are our legs and great comforts they are. They do not cost much, and are kept very cheaply.'

Christmas 1859 was celebrated with great gladness. 'But the great interest of the day was the baptisms in the morning; the grey-headed were there to receive the sign, to seek the grace, to become faithful soldiers and servants of the Lord Jesus. … There were also some young married women, and eight youths from fifteen to nineteen years of age. Their preparation and examination has been extremely interesting to my husband; the boys seem to have grasped the root of the matter and are so happy. It is remarkable in the African character, but one hardly sees anything of sorrow for the past, nor are we able to draw from them that they feel any. They are wonderfully light-hearted people, and when they receive the Gospel, they lay hold of it truly, and renounce heathenism most earnestly, and go on rejoicing.

On the same morning Olubi received a fine Christmas present, another little boy. Little Dan likes him very well, but clings to "Missisi" more than ever; all the week I have washed, fed and done everything for him; he is quite my child.'

When Anna wrote that, you wonder how much she regretted that she had never become a mother. However, considering that Anna's health was precariously fragile, it seems likely that pregnancy in the climate of Africa would have brought disaster for her and her child in the same way that it had for Catherine Bowen (the wife of Bishop John Bowen) who died in 1858 following the stillbirth of their son.

The last comment of 1859 was: 'The school is going on very well. Olubi teaches all the children from nine to twelve, and sometimes my husband or I go in to give a lesson. At twelve, the girls come to me, and Olubi has the boys alone till two; then he is free, but my work goes on with all, one way and the other, till eight o' clock in the evening. I often write till nine, and then go to my room tired, for there is no sleep after half-past five in the morning, and from that time till I go to bed, hardly any rest. I have the comfort of feeling my days are pretty well occupied, though often, it seems, with things of small import, yet those things must be done, and so I desire to possess a quiet and comfortable mind about them.'

The year closed with David still in a very poor state of health. Furthermore a storm which would have frightful consequences was brewing in the locality.

## 1860

In January 1860 Mr. George Jefferies, a lay missionary/evangelist sent by the CMS, arrived at Ibadan to join the team. He was very welcome as David continued to be unwell and was only occasionally able to go out preaching. Not surprisingly, Mr. Jefferies very soon suffered his first attack of fever and needed careful nursing. When he had recovered Anna and David decided to take the opportunity for a break to visit their friends the Townsends at the Mission at Abeokuta. This was to be the last time they were able to be away from Ibadan together for several years but they were unaware of that at the time. Sadly their visit was marred by the disturbing news that Abeokuta was likely to be invaded by the King of Dahomey; therefore a hasty return to Ibadan was necessary.

Before leaving Anna wrote: 'Abeokuta, Sunday Evening, February 19th: We are just now set in the midst of many and great dangers. Dahomey is close upon us! It is said he is not far from the walls, and in the morning an attack is expected. This has been a most anxious trying day, yet the congregation in church was very large, and the Psalms in the morning, and the prayers, were truly comforting, and Mr. Townsend was able to get calmly through a comforting sermon on "I know that my Redeemer liveth." Almost the only peaceful place has been the church. All roads are being shut up, to prevent people from running away. The reports coming in all day are most distressing. I am sorry to say I am terribly upset by it. The anticipation of war unstrings all my nerves. My husband is rather anxious about me, because I have such sudden pains in my left side when the shouts and reports come; and he is determined to take me on the road to Ibadan, if possible, tomorrow. I cannot tell you that I am calm and composed, when I am not; would that it were so! Yet amid the turmoil and disquietude and infirmity of this poor body, I am permitted an undercurrent of peace. I know "This God is our God for ever and ever, He will be our Guide even unto death."'

Another war that was developing was between Ibadan and Ijaye, the town to the north where they had stayed on their way to visit the King of Oyo. The reason for these wars between the numerous Yoruba tribes was very complex and far beyond the scope of this book. There seemed to be few actual battles, but occasional petty skirmishes when people were kidnapped and taken as slaves. An air of hostility seemed to develop where there was normally an atmosphere of cordiality.

'February 28th: We reached home, God be praised, safely, but it was a desolate journey, the road forsaken on account of wars everywhere. We did not know whether we should not be fired upon from the bush any minute, and my poor husband suffered much, but we have every cause to be thankful we came, and our people are glad to have us at home in these troublous times. The sea of life is by no means smoother here than it was in Abeokuta; the chiefs of this place and of Ijaye have quarrelled and caught each other's people, and sold them. Most passionate messages were sent backwards and forwards. Calabashes were presented to one and another, with the request that the chief of Ijaye desires such and such an Ibadan chief's head in that calabash; then these people send back, "We want Are's head in this calabash first." [A calabash is a fruit grown on a vine slightly similar to a gourd. They can be left to grow to an enormous size and used as containers for liquids.]

Now the roads to Ijaye have all been shut, and Ibadan kidnappers have been catching everybody, man, woman, or child, who ventured out in the Ijaye farms. Whether there is to be real war we cannot tell, there are various reports, but it is an anxious time. What a mercy it is when we have grace and faith to lean on the Strong Arm; how truly we can then feel, "I will not fear what man can do unto me."

When you receive this, I hope many of our present anxieties will be over, but you will think of, and pray for us. I cannot tell you how soothed and comforted we often feel, in the remembrance of so many beloved ones praying truly and earnestly for us.'

By the time Anna wrote again a hoped for settlement between the chiefs had not been achieved. 'March 10th: A general war is now proclaimed, and all whose business it is must go. Tremendous sacrifices have been made, and alas on Saturday night, a human sacrifice! A man of about twenty-five or thirty. In the day he was paraded through the markets that people might see what a fine fellow he was; for all the town is taxed to pay the expenses. Some of our people who saw him say that he looked as proud as possible of the honours that awaited him. From being a poor slave, on that day he is all but worshipped, and has the power of saying and doing all he likes, except escaping his death in the evening. But, poor fellow, he believes all kinds of glory await him in the other world, the world of mystery. The moment he is killed, all prostrate themselves in prayer (what prayer!), then follow feasting and rejoicing, and before the body spoils, certain generals must be off on the road to the war. The head of the poor victim is left to the fowls of the air, but the body receives great honour from the women; they rub and decorate it with everything precious, believing that this same man is to return to the world again as an infant, but that he will then, when he grows up, surely be a king. So hundreds of women pay honour to this dead body, each praying she may be the mother when he visits the world again.

Yesterday the people were making other sacrifices at the graves of departed warriors, earnestly entreating their help from the other world. The blindness, the darkness, the foolishness of heathenism! And in the midst of all this we are living; and when pressed down under the thought of these and a thousand other sorrows and horrors, we can hardly help asking sometimes, are we of any use in such a country? But then we are comforted by the thought that beginnings must be made. ... I must finish my letter, for roads all about are shutting, and I may have no opportunity of sending down for the next mail. We have no personal danger to fear, but discomfort enough; no communication with our friends, soon food will be dear, and of course all trade of every kind stopped. Our people are happy to have us remaining quietly amongst them, and we all feel peaceful, having no fear, and go on just as usual.'

'April 1st 1860: I never like writing on Sunday, but as we know of some one going on Monday morning, and in these times opportunities are so rare for sending letters, I gladly spend a little time in communicating with you. Our Sunday services are over, the children's picture lessons ended, and a hearty cheerful singing; and they lie fast asleep on their mats. War troubles are just the same, but we are thankful that food is as yet cheap, and likely to be so for some months, and perhaps then war will be over; but these foolish people like to go on for two or three years and then "sit down" for two or three more. However, we won't think of what they may do; to live a day at a time is the Christian's privilege. My children's appetites do not lessen because of war, and as soon as there were rumours of this time coming, I laid in a large store of yams, palm-oil, and other things, and we have a good stock of cowries.

You think of us, I am sure, in our varied and sometimes trying circumstances. We rejoice in the love and care of our heavenly Father, which we daily and hourly feel in this heathen land, and we thank Him for the gift of so many dear friends at home, to sympathize with and pray for us. I always feel so nearly drawn to you all, on the blessed Sabbath-day, home ties are so strong on this day; there is so much here unlike our home Sabbaths, the language, the people, everything. But oh! it is a blessed day of rest from so many of the secular cares and labours which must attend a missionary life, a time when the mind can be, and is, drawn more towards spiritual things.

I often feel a little tried by the thorough Martha life I am obliged to lead; with twenty children in the house, others out of it, and my husband, who is generally so active, now for many months disabled and suffering, my hands are more than full, and I am afraid my heart too, not in the pleasure of a Martha's life, but in the worry, and cares, and fatigues attending it. Yet I don't see for myself where it is to stop, until the end of the journey, for I am quite sure the more we do the more we find to do. I am very thankful for the health and strength I enjoy; my husband says he looks at me with wonder sometimes. He took a service to-day, after many weeks silence, and got through well; but his health is in a serious critical state; he has now confirmed asthma, which must greatly hinder him in his work.'

Obviously the sailing of the mail steamers from England was not affected by the tribal wars so letters and parcels were being delivered to Lagos, but from there the usual delivery via Abeokuta was unpredictable and very hazardous.

'April 20th: We are going to venture to send some of our people down to Abeokuta next week, as by that time the mail will have arrived, and we want the refreshment of letters from home more than ever in these times, so we must get some letters ready to send down by the same opportunity. It is well white people are yet in favour, for no soul except our very own people could walk that road now, it would be death, and it is very good of our people to venture to do it. There has been a long groaning for war, and now here it is begun; and where is the ending we know not. If it were not for the assurance that our Father in heaven knows all, and will do all things well, and the help He gives us, and little gleams of encouragement in the work, we should be utterly discouraged.'

When the people who had gone to Abeokuta returned they were able to bring some of the boxes that had arrived from England. One was from Mr. Charles Buxton – a son of Sir Thomas and Lady Hannah Buxton – a splendid box of tools. There were more boxes to come when anyone was brave enough to go there again but the menace of kidnappers was ever-present on that route.

It was encouraging that three women came to ask for their names to be put down on the list for baptism. David always had very intensive discussions when people applied in order to discern how genuine they were. He did doubt the sincerity of one of them but the other two were entered on the list as one of them had been attending the church for a year and had heard that a baptism service was soon to be held at which eight babies were to be baptized. These included the second son of Susanna and Olubi who was to be named Jonathan Christmas because he had been born on Christmas Day. Anna and some of the children were busy sewing white gowns and caps for the babies to wear. In those days babies often wore a cap with a bird embroidered on it, symbolizing the dove of peace descending as at the baptism of Jesus. On Ascension Day they held an evening service and after that an evening service was held every week.

In June Mr. Jefferies was able to move into his own house about two miles away across the town where it was hoped that another church would one day be built. An African teacher had already been living there for a while and sowing the seeds of the Christian gospel.

The following extracts from Anna's letters indicate their awareness of the surrounding disturbances and the preparations for coping with the situation: 'August 7th: Our war position is much the same, yet a little worse, which is rather a relief, as it gives hope of a quicker end. We have a wonderful in-gathering in Ibadan, yams and cora, beyond all our expectations a few months ago; so that we have plenty of food, and not dear; but our people are troubled for want of cowries, and we have to open our store in faith; and hope that they will last till peace comes. European comforts, and what in a general way appear and are necessaries, we must do without, and be thankful for what yet remains in our hand. With tea, coffee, sugar, we think ourselves rich, and are glad to be able to share them with Mr. Jeffries. What we shall most regret is our flour, when that is gone. You can soon be weary of yams, if you have to take them as the staff of life. But by Christmas we hope war will be over.'

'August 11th: It looks dark indeed, just now. … The work is also going on; only four of our church people are in the war, and they were obliged to go; and we have newcomers, and three of the greatest persecutors, two women and a man, have joined the class of candidates for baptism, and the man is to be baptized soon, with eleven or twelve others. Our children are all going on very steadily and amiably. My dear husband still suffers much, but he is thankful to be able to get on as well as he does; his presence is very necessary at this time. I continue in excellent health, and am very busy, and we are permitted to sing a joyful song of praise and thanksgiving unto our Father and our Redeemer, who has called us here, and makes us happy.'

'October 13th: I must write and yet have little inclination. Our future looks very dark. Today we hear that our only coast-road is going to be shut. This threat may blow over, as others have done; but it looks more real now. … We are weary with war, sounds of war, talks of war, anticipations of war; but we have been mercifully kept and comforted. Another feature has appeared; our farms in all directions are troubled with kidnappers. If this goes on, we may be troubled for food. I have been obliged in faithfulness to tell you some of our dark side, but we are thankful for some signs of a brighter one, and we do rejoice too in our way and our work, and are permitted to know what it is to be sorrowful, yet always rejoicing. God be praised we do not work in a desponding mood.'

The road to the coast was closed and as fewer letters were likely to be collected fewer letters were written. Communication with the outside world became very tenuous for the next few months. The first major problem was the shortage of cowries which they needed daily to buy the food that could not be grown at the Mission. Once the road was closed the travelling traders no longer came and therefore there was no one willing to exchange dollars for cowries. Although David had thought that he had sufficient stored to last a long time the prospect of running out grew ever more real.

When Christmas came they held their usual services but the festivities had to be curtailed. 'We could not afford it,' wrote Anna, 'but the day was made bright to the children, and the Christians were full of sympathy, and assembled in goodly numbers in church, washed, and oiled, and dressed in their very best, their woolly hair freshly plaited (which sometimes is not done for months together), and looking as cheerful as possible; and they parted, having passed a blessed, happy day.'

How were they to survive without cowries to pay for the items they needed? On 31st December David decided to ask for help from the local chiefs and therefore went to visit them at their war camp leaving Anna in charge of the household, which by this time numbered 70 people. In her journal Anna wrote: 'December 31st: The last hours of this year of years are now fast drawing to a close, my children gone to sleep, my husband in the camp, and I have had a quiet day. Wonderful have been the mercies of this year of trial; sad have been the wars and fightings about us. Oh, we have a cup of sorrow to drink; but no more of this; only Thou, O God, have pity upon us! We have had no communication with anyone outside Ibadan for three months, and no mail for three months, a grievous loss, especially as there was no letter by the last from my dearest friend, the vicar [Francis Cunningham]. I am hungry to hear of my dear friends, but almost more anxious for them to hear of us; they will all be thinking of us in our war calamities in a heathen land. But I pray God to comfort them concerning us, and to keep them all in peace in the hollow of His hand, as He so mercifully does us, in the midst of all our troubles.

Farewell, 1860! All the sins and sorrows, all the omissions and commissions, I take to my merciful Saviour, and lay them at the foot of the Cross … Give me grace to live to Thee, to love and serve Thee in this dark land. …'

## 1861

'January 1st 1861: We have had a nice day, and in some measure I enjoy beginning a new year; but I miss my ever dear kind husband. How often we are separated at Christmas or New Year. Even on our visit to England it was so; but we are one in heart and meet in spirit, when absent in the body. Whenever he is away, it is in the path of duty. My heart's fervent desire is that our dear Lord and Master's work may flourish in Ibadan this year.'

Not knowing whether the letter would ever be sent, Anna wrote to the Reverend Francis Cunningham on January 4th 1861: 'D. having to go to the camp on December 31st wrote an address for Olubi to deliver in his name on New Year's Day, which he did very well. We met together in the morning. Three persons prayed, and we sang hymns, and the address was given; in this way we started our new year, hoping you were engaged in much the same manner in one of your schoolrooms and that we might be bearing one another on our hearts before our heavenly Father, at pretty much the same time; you gathering together in the dark and cold, we in the glaring sunshine of Africa; but each and all in our right places, where our wise and loving Father would have us to be. …' No doubt they sang the missionary hymn, "Jesus shall reign" with great conviction.

'We are quite shut up by war, but are always hoping we shall soon be in a better condition. Our God has been wonderfully gracious to us in preserving our health and spirits. My dear husband often suffers much with his cough, but he is not worse, and just now he is very much better. I have gone on with remarkable health, sometimes worn and weary with work and cares, as many a labourer is in dear old England; and of course all things are increased in wear and weight in a climate like this, but, God be praised, I have no illness. Our living is rather poor at this time; we cook yams in all sorts of ways, to make them palatable. I can eat palaver sauce and beans. D. cannot, but he likes Indian corn-flour made into porridge, which I do not, so we get on very fairly. There is plenty of this kind of food in the town, but our great trouble is the want of cowries, for, in the present state of things, there are no traders from whom we may buy them.

Here we all are - ourselves, Mr. Jeffries, our school, our native teachers, in all seventy persons - and everyone has for more than two months eaten, and is now eating, from our store of cowries which we were enabled to lay in. That store is now nearly exhausted, though we have been as careful as possible, only allowing our two selves a pennyworth of meat in our soup, and glad to eat beans, with a little onion and pepper to flavour them, and pinching in the salt as if it were gold dust; but we have plenty of its kind to eat, and there is no poverty among the natives yet.'

Her journal in February tells, 'Our work in general goes on steadily, but war is not conducive to its progress; the people are wild, restless, and unsettled. Mr. Hinderer's appeal for help had been received by the chiefs with many expressions of regard for his character and useful work, and of willingness to grant his request. But Ifa (their god) must be consulted and a few days later the answer was given that Ifa forbade them to lend the white man cowries; and, though a present of cowries was shortly afterwards received from the head chiefs, such help could not be expected again.'

The chief, Bale, who had enjoyed visiting them in their new house and obviously regarded them as friends, could not be asked for help as he was seriously ill with paralysis which proved to be terminal.

The African teachers and all the members of the Mission were dependent on them for their salaries which were sent from the mission at Abeokuta. What could they do next?

Well, they had things they could possibly sell in the market at Ibadan. So they searched the house for anything that might raise a few cowries. They found some old tin match boxes and old biscuit boxes. They sold well.

What about the lead linings from the wooden boxes in which they had brought their possessions from England? They took those out carefully and the children had a marvellous time helping to polish them to look as valuable as possible. These proved to be very popular.

Later they sold household utensils that were not in regular use and then even sold some of their clothes.

The Christians knew about the problems and one of them gave them two bags of cowries. However, most of the Christians were poor and could not afford to help them. The non-Christians were not aware of the situation. It seemed that most of the compounds had a garden plot making the household self sufficient for food

Olubi's aunt, who was not a Christian, lent them two bags and there were other small gifts for which they were immensely grateful. But other things had to be considered.

By this time they had been for more than six months without flour and Anna and David were living on a handful of horse beans and the produce of their garden so that they were able to feed the children as well as possible. Being on a near starvation diet did them no good and both were in increasingly poor health. In later years they admitted to having sometimes cried themselves to sleep with hunger.

In a letter of March 4th Anna wrote: 'All my children who have parents or homes I have sent away to-day, making arrangements with them for the purpose; and we were comforted by the nice way in which the people took it. One woman offered to take one of my children, who has no other home, in order to help us; we have now tried all ways and means, but little is left in hand. We have tried to borrow, but none will lend; they say, and very naturally, "We cannot tell how long this war may last; it may be finished in a few weeks, or it may last some years." … These poor heathen say, "God will not and cannot suffer us to want, and truly in Him do we trust."

Some poor heathens look on and say, "What is the use of their serving God? They die, and they get trouble." The Mohammedans say, God loves us very well, but we do not worship Him the right way, and do not give honour to His prophet. … We do sometimes think of what might be, if these people were really to turn against us, but we are wonderfully delivered from fear of evil.

We had the comfort of getting our three months' mails in January, and a few days ago we received your letters written in December. Thus we have had all the 1860 letters so do not be discouraged about writing; we shall get them somehow or other, and think of the refreshment they must be to us.'

One day when Anna was standing outside their gate because she could not bear to watch the children eating a hearty meal, she greeted in Yoruba a woman passing by carrying on her head a bunch of Indian corn. The woman was surprised to hear her native language being spoken by a white woman and stopped to talk to Anna to ask how this came about. Anna explained how she came to be in Ibadan and why she had come. Then the woman gave Anna a handful of her corn which Anna gratefully took and roasted for herself and David.

Milk was something they regularly bought but in view of the shortage of cowries the order was for less and less. The friendly woman, who delivered it, realizing that something was amiss, questioned Anna. When she heard of their predicament she said that they must send the usual order every day. Eventually Anna had enough cowries to be able to repay her, but she very firmly refused to take the money.

With so many people dependent on them for survival Anna and David discussed at length how to deal with the problem. Finally they decided that David must make the extremely risky journey to Lagos as there was simply no other way of obtaining cowries. Also, David's quarterly allowances from the CMS would have been waiting for collection, so, on 6th March, David and two of the oldest boys in great faith and courage set out on the four day, 80 mile trek to Lagos, taking with them just a few clothes and enough food for the journey. None of the older men would go for fear of kidnappers. Fortunately they did not meet anyone on the journey and reached Lagos in safety. Having made the required business arrangements to procure cowries, David heard of a caravan of traders going to Ibadan and thought they would be safe travelling back with them. He gave one of the traders money to be exchanged for cowries once they had reached Ibadan and also sent a load of flour and other provisions that they needed. However, on March 29th, the day he should have travelled, he was extremely ill and unable to mount his horse and so the caravan went without him and the boys.

After the caravan had gone some distance, it was ambushed and the goods being carried were plundered and a great many people were killed, because the King of the Ijebu had heard that David might be travelling with the traders and he intended to kill him. Not finding David further infuriated the King of the Ijebu who was more than ever determined to kill him. He sent word to David and to the British Consul saying that 'If the white man goes back to Ibadan, he will surely take off his head, as he cannot sell a white man'.

Now with a price on his head David was in a quandary. His illness at Lagos was a blessing in disguise as he was carefully nursed by the Reverend and Mrs. Maser, the missionaries there, and seen by a doctor and for a few weeks had good food. Gradually he recovered enough strength to ride again and with much prayer Anna tells that: 'at last he felt "There is no road for me but the Ijebu road, and by that I must go; and after all, my time is in God's hand, and not in the Ijebu king's", so he started with his two boys, on the track through the bush for Ibadan. Along the track they and the horse were terrified at the sight of the remains of the slaughtered travellers who had been in the caravan and they could see smoke from distant fires of the Ijebus who may have left the track to shelter from a torrential rain storm. But they plodded on.

When darkness fell on the last day they stopped for the night in a shack where the exhausted boys immediately fell asleep but David was too disturbed to more than doze because he could hear the eerie rustling of a snake in the roof thatch. As soon as it was light they journeyed on and soon were in sight of Ibadan. People had been watching for them and a great shout of joy went up when they were seen approaching. David was by that time in a desperately weak state and at the Mission had to be lifted off his horse and lovingly carried into the house. Anna's journal of April 29th said simply, 'My beloved husband came home safely, having escaped many dangers, through God's great mercy. Oh, what thankfulness fills our home again!' Apparently when the King of Ijebu heard that David had reached home in safety, he declared that it was God who had protected the white man, and none but God!

In the next letter Anna wrote; 'May 3rd: I begin with the joyful news that my dear husband is safe at home once more in Ibadan. He arrived last Monday, to my great surprise, and very great thankfulness, but he is now in bed, in much suffering and fever. But how he has suffered in Lagos! If he had had such an illness here, he must have sunk, and even now it is sad to see him, so broken-down and worn.

It was a happy day, indeed. The news flew like lightning through the town, and our house was crammed by the converts and others, truly rejoicing. It reached the war-camp also, and the next day we had several messages from the chiefs and others of our friends. There was such an excitement, because all had heard of the king of Ijebu's intention to kill him. I was the only one who did not know it.'

Then she told how she really coped with her anxiety: 'One day especially, it had been such a day of hope and expectation, but the evening closed in without its realization; and the disappointment was so great that I went to my room and wept bitterly, mind and body being exhausted ….'

A few weeks later Anna wrote, 'My poor husband was sadly unequal to such a journey; excitement and anxiety lent him strength to get through it, but another illness attacked him immediately, and for thirty days he has been fearfully ill. But he was so thankful to be at home, and I to have him, that we could feel nothing but thankfulness. He is, I trust, in some measure recovering now, but he is sadly broken down, and often thinks his days for work in this climate are numbered. Sometimes we feel we should like to go in search of some health, which is so sadly denied him here; but the door is so entirely shut upon us, that I feel thankful that he is happy in its being his Lord's will that he should remain at his post, and that he has no craving to get away, but hopes for some measure of strength to go on; and it is a comfort to us to feel we are of real use in keeping things together, though he is often so sadly afflicted. I cannot be thankful enough for my own health, and that we are both favoured with good spirits. My work is never done, and the days never long enough, and God's love and mercy are great.

The affection, attention, and kindness of our people and our native teachers, in this whole time of trouble, while my husband was away, and now in his sickness, have been really cheering and comforting to us. One of the men, not yet baptized, though cowries are scarce in his hand, sent us a bag of cowries for joy that his minister had come home again.

We have not much missionary news to tell, in these sad times of war. All minds are set on its troubles and excitements, but we are thankful our church is but little shaken by it. Very few, not more than four, have been obliged to go into the war, but we have no new convert this year. My dear children have been very good lately. Their conduct, habits and desires have much improved. I have laboured to make these children industrious, whether at work or play. … I have been really repaid this year. They have known our trouble for want of cowries, and felt our every endeavour that they should not want and have done everything to help me. I have not bought one bit of wood this year, they have gone in the afternoons and fetched of their own accord, which at another time they would not have thought of doing; they wash the clothes for the whole school, and do many such things. It seems a small thing to write, but it has really pleased and comforted me.

We have the prospect of a plentiful harvest, which begins to be reaped this month, and our burden is lighter respecting our people and teachers, as we made them all plant for themselves, so they will get corn this month, and yams next, which will feed them for some time. I am thankful to have some flour for my dear husband that was saved from the great losses.

There is a good deal of earnest prayer, I believe, called forth in Ibadan in this war-season. The natives regularly hold a daily meeting at six o' clock, and there is a tone and spirit in it which there was not before. Then there are the Monday evening meetings, and our monthly prayer meetings, and also on a Wednesday afternoon our teachers all meet, with a few of the most earnest and true of the converts, and what gives us comfort and hope of their being heard is, that the spirit is so different from what it was at first.

On June 30th, we had a very interesting baptism of eighteen children. A few were infants, others our day-school children, and five of my own special charge. I think it was a season of good to us, they appeared solemnized, and expressed very nice and simple desires. The congregation was much impressed, and the eyes of some mothers standing round glistened with a teardrop. They were an imposing sight in their white garments.'

'August 1st: There is a chance again of communicating with dear friends in England. A few days ago we had the joy of receiving our month's mail, letters written in April. … .I have more than enough to do in the common and uncommon business of African life, such work having lately increased for me, in having to look after the growing, as well as the using, of food. We are still in our cowry scarcity, and must be till the war is over; but we are wonderfully helped on by little presents of yams and corn, and by disposing of things.'

One of the next things to be disposed of was Anna's beautifully warm voluminous woollen cloak 'which I cannot wear except on the voyage home. I got 20,000 cowries for it (about £1), much less than it is worth, but the cowries are worth more to us now than six times the value at another time, so we laugh and say we have all been living on Iya's cloak.'

Among her skills and talents Anna proved herself to be a very 'green-fingered' gardener. 'This week we are living on the proceeds of my onion beds. Onions are much used here, and I determined by a little care to try and improve on my beds, and I have had fine ones. One of our church people sells them for us. It is wonderful how we get on all this time, and where we should be glad of five bags (about £5), are made content with five strings of cowries (5d).'

In one of the last letters of 1861 Anna said 'It is quite possible we may spend Christmas, 1862, in England, but if this war lasts twenty years, we cannot get away! Many people ask, why do we not go down, as we are so sick, etc? But even if we our two selves could escape on the road of danger how can we leave our children, our native teachers and their families, in all this trouble?'

## 1862

Anna's letter of January 1st 1862 said: 'Your kind hearts are, I well know, longing for tidings of us. We are weary for letters also, having had none since those written in June ; we cannot help longing for home letters to perfect our New Year's Day, but we hope soon for the great treat of receiving the July, August, September and October mails, and some dollars to buy cowries with, for our daily needs.

1861 has passed away with its cares, sorrows, pains, and though last, not least, its many mercies; 1862 has commenced; we sometimes think it looks sad, dark and heavy, and we fear to tread it, but we know who is the same yesterday, to-day, and for ever, through war, sickness, all things, yes, through death itself. This has been the subject of my husband's address at our early morning service. There is a prayer meeting every morning at six or earlier, but on this morning we have it at seven, to give time for our people who are far off in this large town, and all came so bright and happy, truly enjoying it. They were here long before seven, for kind greetings, good words, and blessings. My thoughts and musings are many on this day, but I must come to our matter-of-fact history, especially as I have only three thin sheets of paper besides this. War, so-called war, is still going on, with very little of real war, but roads shut up and parties out kidnapping. We, of the mission in Ibadan, are the chief and almost the only sufferers; depending on the coast as we do….' Here is the first inkling of another problem looming for Anna and David, one that perhaps would not have been anticipated.

'European necessaries and comforts we have long been without, and cannot have again. My last pair of shoes are on my feet, and my clothes are so worn and so few, that if the war does not end soon, I shall have to come to a country cloth, and roll up like a native. These would be small troubles if we were in health, but my dear husband is a sad sufferer and every bit of remedy or alleviation, in the way of medicine, has been for some months entirely finished. I have had two most severe attacks of fever, one in August, and one in November. I only began to get out on Christmas Day, to the great pleasure of our people, who said it would be no Christmas at all if I were not with them. And I have been getting better ever since, creeping up hill and falling by degrees into all my various duties; but recovering is slow work, when even a cup of tea can now only be taken sparingly, by way of a luxury, as very little is left. Goat meat and yams, though good enough at other times, are not very nourishing or congenial now, and the season is fearfully hot. We do sometimes feel weary and cast down, and then cheer and comfort are given; we are mercifully helped on from day to day.'

'March 3rd: On the 13th February came our precious six months mails. I had fifty letters for my share, and how happy was I. We are most fortunate, in all this war and confusion, that up to this time we have received all our letters from home. There has been much small-pox among our school-children, but all are going on nicely, it is made nothing of in this country; it has been raging in the town this year, and we know of only one death.'

Much resourcefulness was needed when one of the girls broke her arm. However, Anna's First Aid skills were able to provide a solution. 'On January 10th, one of my little girls fell from some steps outside our house, broke the inner bone of the arm, and dislocated the wrist. We did our best to put it to rights immediately; and because we could not make splints, and did not like to wait, my husband cut up the strong board cover of a German book, and I bandaged it up. My lotion was vinegar and water, and all went on admirably. The third night she was in dreadful pain, but after that she had no more. Those first nights I was very anxious about her, not trusting my surgical doings; so I never left her, and would not let any one touch her but myself for three days. After that, she was very happy in my room, with her picture-book and doll; and when I released the bandages she could again move her hand quite freely. I was greatly surprised at the perfect cure; all now to be seen is that the wrist is a little thicker than the other. So we have been helped over this trouble.

I must tell you of a most useful gift. I have three pairs of new shoes! American shoes too, and from further in the interior. An American Baptist missionary sent me them from Oyo; they were his dear wife's, who died four years ago, after having been less than three months in Africa. Thus our daily wants are supplied, even in such a matter as shoes.

The war has been a sad hindrance to us in many a way; preventing the completion of the second station in this town, where Mr. Jeffries is residing, and also the making of a third station, where a native teacher [Henry Johnson] lives. We have managed to build a little house for him and his family lately; he was only in a borrowed room in a large compound, and that was not so pleasant; but as we and he have all helped, we made it for very few cowries, and it will be well worth what it has cost, even if we have to make the proper place next year. We sadly want the opening of the roads which the end of this war will bring; my children are so out of clothes, such a shabby little party they are, and there are so many nice boxes waiting for us, clothes, books, and slates, &c.; when I think of it all, I am sure we shall not have time to go home. I am nicely well; if only my dear husband should get as well!'

When the town of Ijaye was dangerously threatened by the tribal conflict there, the missionaries, Mr. and Mrs. Mann, were escorted to safety by a party led by Lieutenant Dolben. At the mission was also a lay evangelist - Edward Roper. He decided to stay on at Ijaye. However, when Ijaye was captured in March 1862 he was taken prisoner and treated very brutally. Ijaye, with about 50,000 inhabitants, was completely destroyed and within a year it was completely ruinous and overgrown.

David Hinderer, knowing of the plight of Edward Roper who was imprisoned in Ibadan, persuaded the tribal chiefs to release him. They did so on condition that he lived with Anna and David at the Ibadan Mission 'on parole'.

Anna's next letter shows that, courageously, they carried on the routine of their lives. 'May 30th: We are living just as we can, others helping us, out of their poverty. We get a yam here, and a yam there, and a little corn in the same manner. One of our converts yesterday lent us some cowries, which must, by pinching, last us three or four weeks, if possible; he had to borrow them from a heathen friend, before he could lend them to us. Dearest friends, you will think of us, and long to help us, but there is nothing left for your kind hearts to do for us, but to pray.'

Anna often thought of little schemes like the following that would provide a distraction and brighten life at the Mission: 'August 15th. I have a corner in the piazza, which I call my study. It is a funny little place, but very pleasant to me. Here I read and write and receive any favoured visitors. Where there is wall, it is washed with a kind of red earth, but where it is of boards, they are very rough, and overlap one another. I took it into my head a little while ago to ornament it, for an amusement, and to enjoy it afterwards; so out of an old London News I have got some pretty English scenes, domestic groups, children, and animals, all of which are an immense delight to my little and big children, and form a never-ending subject of conversation when they are admitted there.'

Later that year Mr. Jeffries had to return to stay at the Mission house as he was desperately ill again with fever and needed expert nursing. Sadly he died on 22nd September and early the next morning he was buried by lamplight in the little Kudeti churchyard. This left his house vacant. Therefore Mr. Roper was glad to go to live there and to serve at the Ogunpa station of the Ibadan Mission some two miles away from Kudeti.

As David's health was still giving a great deal of concern and he was not often able to go out preaching, he took the opportunity to use his time and energy doing translation work. 'November 17th: My husband is much interested in translating [into Yoruba] the Pilgrim's Progress. We indulge in the hope of taking it home to print before long and we think it will be particularly interesting and useful to our Africans. This work has been a great pleasure to him, and helps to reconcile him to the quiet life he has been obliged to lead of late. Through God's mercy, I do not think I have had even a day's ailing since last November. Pray for us, and give thanks also, for God's mercy endureth for ever.'

'December 9th: We and our people have sold everything which we can turn into money and the thought and burden of all that is upon us is getting almost more than we can bear. A few days ago I did get cast down, but our gracious God was merciful to us, as He ever is; our troubles are many, but His support is mighty. My dear husband's state is most serious; some nights ago he had hours of fearful coughing, and every moment seemed as if it might be his last; and we have not the least, the simplest, remedy to relieve him. He was much exhausted for two or three days, and one of our people, who could ill afford it, brought us a bag of cowries (about one pound's worth), and told us to take it and use it freely to buy meat and more strengthening things than beans, &c., which we are generally content with. That bag of cowries, which was to have been for our comfort, and especially for my poor husband, we had to give up, to rescue the daughter of the scripture-reader of Awaye from being sold. [She had been captured by the Ibadan people.] I nearly cried, yet we were thankful we had it, and could thus rescue the poor girl; and so gracious, and merciful, and faithful has our God been, that we have, after all, been living better than for some time past.

We sold a counterpane, and a few yards of damask which had been overlooked by us; so that we indulge every now and then in one hundred cowries worth of meat (about one pennyworth), and such a morsel seems like a little feast to us in these days. I have been buying today ten baskets of corn, and hope to buy five more to-morrow, for our children especially; and I was sadly afraid I could not even buy one basket in store this season; and so, time after time, is our want of faith put to shame and also our faith revived and strengthened. Those baskets of corn are such a delightful sight to me this evening that I can scarcely help running just to take a look at them, and be thankful.

I have made out an almanac, by the help of the Prayer-book; I shall gladly throw it away if the proper ones reach us by some good chance. This letter, if it reaches you, will have gone from here to Lagos such a roundabout way, twenty-five days journey at least, instead of three; but these people are inveterate traders and walkers; where they can buy and sell, there is not a distance which will prevent their going.'

At the end of December Anna and David were greatly cheered to have three visitors, Captain James Pinson Lapulo Davies and the Reverend James Lamb from Lagos and the Reverend Buhler from Abeokuta. They came on a mission of peace and to discover at first-hand how the situation was at Ibadan. With whom they negotiated for peace is unclear but they were unsuccessful. At least they were able to see the seriousness of David's ill health and how the shortage of cowries was affecting their lives. Did they leave them with a further supply of cowries? Capt. Pinson was the son of former slaves. He had become a CMS teacher and later joined the British Royal Navy on one of the anti-slavery ships before becoming a very successful merchant in Lagos. The Revd. James Lamb was the English priest of a church in Lagos.

Lagos became a British Colony on 5th March 1862 with Capt. John Hawley Glover R.N. as the Governor/Administrator from August 1863. When he heard of the plight of the missionaries at Ibadan, he was unstinting in his efforts to help them but the King of the Ijebus absolutely refused to allow him or anyone sent by him to pass through his territory. Perhaps the King's attitude is understandable. Maybe he had reasons for his hostility to the British. He probably considered that they had virtually invaded his country and destroyed much of his trade - particularly in slaves.

## 1863

From the beginning of 1863 letters were occasionally delivered safely to Ibadan but were often delayed and packets and parcels were intercepted and vanished. Outgoing letters became very few and possibly some of those went astray too. There was less and less will to write, leading to greater and greater isolation. Another problem arose which might have been difficult to anticipate - they were rapidly running out of paper. For people used to spending many hours each day in writing sermons and notes for sermons, and translating books and writing letters, this was indescribable misery. Anna and David told in later years how they searched for every scrap of paper that could be used – like the fly leaves of printed books and blank pages from half-used books, some of them already part eaten by the white ants. Maybe the unused pages from Anna's journal were used which would explain the lack of entries after 1862.

School lessons had to be curtailed because many of the slates had become cracked with use over the years and the replacements had not arrived. The sewing classes for the girls had to be discontinued because the only resources left were two rusty needles and part of one ball of cotton. These had to be preserved for Anna's use in an emergency.

'March 16th 1863: We live a day at a time; we eat to-day, and trust for to-morrow. The prayer, "Give us this day our daily bread," is not unanswered. All are busy planting their farms, and, thank God! there is a good prospect of plenty of food; rains are beginning, and corn already, five days after planting, shoots up, and in June we shall be eating it. We feel your prayers are answered every day on our behalf, in the care and love and presence and comfort given. We are not yet delivered, but kept and even comforted in our trial in a land of captivity.'

'September 29th: In August we had the joy of receiving precious packets of letters, and with them dollars and calico, and things to sell for cowries, and a little tea, and other comforts for ourselves. Food too is plentiful, and very cheap, and cowries are much more in circulation than last year, so we feel quite rich again, and I hope truly thankful. It is an utter impossibility for us to get away till this war is ended, and I see no chance of that now; but being so mercifully helped again, I hope we are enabled to bear our trials better, and are more cheerful and happy than we were inclined to be a year ago; and oh, it is such a comfort, we are sent here, put here. We met with some lines by [Richard Chenevix] Trench, on Sunday evening, which were quite refreshing; they begin thus:

"Thou cam'st not to thy place by accident,<br>
It is the very place God meant for thee,<br>
And should'st thou here small scope for action see,<br>
Do not for this give room to discontent."

And so here we are. The Lord give us to feel the privilege of doing or suffering His holy will. Six years, next month, since we left England this last time. I wonder how many more it may be before we see it again.'

## 1864

'March 22nd 1864: I have a new occupation now. About seven weeks ago a little babe of a about six months was put out by a brook in some grass; whether because it is a slave, or its mother died, or an idol priest ordered it, we have no idea. No one in the whole town would dare to take it, and it remained there three nights and days, in the night shrieking bitterly (which effectually frightened the wild beasts away), in the day comforted by every mother who passed by giving it suck. As soon as we heard of it, we took it, and are bringing it up by hand. It has been quite ill from all the changes and the night dew giving it cough, so that our poor little baby gives us much trouble and anxiety. As she will only take to myself and my eldest girl, she fills my hands extremely. She is very passionate, but when better, she can laugh with us, and seems clinging. We love her very much. We call her Eyila, which means 'this has escaped' or 'is saved'.

Oh, dearest friends, this sad war will not let us meet. I did hope by this spring-time to be in your midst; but our Father knows where we are, and why; I am thankful for the gift of a more reconciled spirit, submissive to all, feeling that His hand, His providence, is at work, though we may seem in the dark sometimes, and tried, and tossed, and discouraged.'

'November 18th: About five weeks since I had such an attack of fever as I should have thought only a newcomer could have had, and such as I have not had for some years. I thought at one time I was to have a short journey home, the gates of which, through the love and mercy of Jesus, no one could shut. I wonder that I should have liked coming back to the storms and sorrows of life, but I did like the thought of working in better times in this country, and my dear husband seemed to want me, and a few people and children in Ibadan; and I should like to reach England once more first, and see dear friends and faces, and get refreshed in body and soul, and then to come back to work with fresh heart and zeal. We do get so cast down at times, we are so let and hindered in our work, our hearts faint, and our hands hang down.

No materials for our schools, not even a Bible for each child, and we have such hard work and toil in only just holding things together; yet again we are comforted in the thought that we are not altogether useless, and we are enabled in the dark hour to stay ourselves upon our God, and receive innumerable helps and comforts from Him, our faithful covenant-keeping God. And we are very cheerful too, though sorrowful some times. My little black boys and girls are doing well on the whole, and my blackest of black babies is very flourishing, and a real pleasure to us, always ready to come to 'Iya'. She can call me 'Iya' now, though she makes no farther progress in talking and none in walking, her feet are so tiny. She could not understand my being ill when I could not take her. She would sit on my bed and play, and if I say, "Kiss Iya," she throws her pretty little arms round me, and kisses me, and laughs, as much amused.'

## 1865

'January 14th 1865: Because there is only time to write a scrap, and my heart longs to send you a letter, I am almost tempted to leave it for a better opportunity, but I do not like that either; so I send just what I can, and not what I would. Just now we hear of a person starting in an hour for Lagos, how or where we cannot tell, and I sit down for many such like scraps to let our dear and anxious friends hear of us, though we have no better news.

We are both very poorly, so exhausted by the long stay, and we cannot get out till war is done and it is such a sickly, dry season; we feel sometimes so weak in the morning, after a night of fever, that we say, "Well, this day we must do nothing, but just try to keep ourselves alive," but the day brings its work, and with it its cheer sometimes, as well as its care, and we rejoice in the evening coolness. We have had close and private examination and conversation with our dear people, at the close of 1864, and are much cheered and comforted, though we add none to our numbers. Our young men are truly hopeful. We see much of a real work of grace in their hearts.'

This was probably the last letter sent from Ibadan that year as at nightfall one April evening a mysterious band of visitors arrived at the Mission. When they explained why they had come there must have been considerable consternation in the Mission House. Their leader was a fearless young Captain Maxwell who had been sent with a party of carefully chosen reliable men to carry out specific instructions from the Governor of Lagos. They had been told to cut a new slightly longer overland route through the dense and fast growing bush to Ibadan and make an immediate return with the Hinderer missionaries before the new track could be discovered. They were equipped with food for the journey and a hammock for Anna.

All at the Mission were totally unprepared for this shock. A decision had to be made extremely quickly as they needed to leave again at daybreak – about 5.00 a.m. – in order not to be discovered. Could David, as the priest in charge of an extensive missionary enterprise, just walk away from the work like that? What were their responsibilities to themselves and to the others at the Mission? What would happen after their departure? How would the Mission continue? If they did not take this chance, when would there be another?

By 10.00 p.m. it had been decided. David knew that he could not possibly leave at such short notice, even though for his health an opportunity to go to the coast, and eventually to England, was extremely desirable. He knew that to delegate his responsibilities needed rather more thoughtful planning, even though he had the greatest confidence in the African staff that he had been carefully training for several years. Anna's situation was different. The organization of the household could be taken over by those who normally shared the duties with her. She realized that she should take the opportunity to leave in the hope that David would be able to follow as soon as appropriate arrangements could be made. She spent the night collecting together a few essential things and giving instructions for the carrying out of the household duties she normally did.

Konigbagbe (from Oyo), who by this time had been Anna's personal maid for several years, was insistent that she should go to Lagos with Anna. But was this a good idea? Although she was fully grown she was totally unused to bush walking. Did she even have shoes to wear? However she had grown into a feisty and determined young woman, so it was agreed that she should go and she quickly packed her belongings in a bundle to be carried on her head. It was decided that the children must not be told until the little party had left because their farewells to 'Iya' would have been too distressing for anyone to cope with.

Anna's feelings on contemplating the journey to Lagos, and eventually to England, are not known. However, considering that she rode around the town on her pony, and seldom walked very far, the journey to Lagos was going to be an enormous challenge. Were her shoes suitable for a trek through the bush? Furthermore, for the journey to England she no longer possessed the warm cloak that had been such a comfort on previous voyages. Was she apprehensive about the seasickness she had previously suffered from? How did she feel about leaving David? When would they ever meet again? She already knew that Francis Cunningham had died. Who would greet her on arrival in England? She probably did not even know at which port she might disembark. David's feelings are also unknown. It was a tremendous challenge for both of them but, as always, they knew in whom they put their trust.

When daylight came many children awoke early, probably sensing that something unusual was happening, so there was a very tearful farewell as the little party set off with Anna being carried in the hammock. For much of the journey the track was far too narrow for that and Anna just had to walk. In places the undergrowth had already grown back across the track making it slightly uncertain which was the path. A swift pace of walking had to be maintained in spite of the terrain. Poor Konigbagbe had never had to walk like that before, but she was very uncomplaining and brave about the pain she had to bear from her feet which became severely cut and swollen. As they journeyed, in places they could hear the voices of Ijebus as they passed near to them but they silently hurried on, arriving at Lagos on the fourth day, hungry, worn and weary but with immensely thankful hearts that they had completed the journey safely.

# Chapter 7 The second home leave 1865 to 1866

At Lagos, Konigbagbe stayed with Anna until 10th April when Anna embarked on the next ship to England. That was the *S.S. Macgregor Laird* bound for Liverpool. After a sad farewell, Konigbagbe returned to Ibadan where she became a most valued member of the Christian community.

The *Macgregor Laird* carrying Anna sailed into Liverpool on 13th May 1865. However it was another two months before David arrived in England having arranged for the Ibadan Mission to be in the care of the Revd. Joseph Smith and his wife Ellen, who had been at the Badagry Mission. Anna and David's first days together were spent in London reporting to the Church Missionary Society and dealing with other business.

Research has not revealed details of where they went after that. However, in the autumn they went to stay with their friends at Halesowen Rectory. Whilst there, David was concentrating on his translation of *Pilgrims Progress* into Yoruba. He was also translating English hymns into Yoruba and writing others in Yoruba in order to produce a book of hymns. David's health seemed to be giving even more concern than Anna's and they were advised to spend the winter in the south of England. They stayed for the first two months of 1866 at Dawlish where they made new friends and were warmly welcomed. The church at Dawlish generously gave a harmonium for the church at Ibadan and clothes and other gifts for the children at the Mission.

From Dawlish they went to Bedford and then to various friends in Norfolk before going to Lowestoft where so much had changed since their last visit.

Although there appears not to have been any mention of it in Anna's letters from Ibadan, the Revd. Francis Cunningham had died in 1863. In his will he left many generous bequests to charitable causes in Lowestoft and to Anna he left £200 – a very considerable amount of money in those days. Correspondence deposited in Lowestoft Record Office includes a letter sent by Anna from Ibadan to Francis Cunningham's solicitor saying that she was most concerned that part of this money should be used to support one of her young half-brothers whilst doing an apprenticeship and some spent to help Miss Toll who must have been a family friend. From the correspondence available, it seems that other letters between Anna and the solicitor went astray. One of the executors of Francis Cunningham's will was the Revd. William Ripley, who had been his assistant curate at Lowestoft.

Throughout their leave a steady flow of letters came to Anna and David from Ibadan, keeping them firmly in touch with the happenings at home there. One contained the sad news of the death of Arubo who been at the Mission school for eleven years since they rescued him from starvation. Another gave news of the death in March from smallpox of Eyila whom Anna had nurtured to health as a very tiny abandoned baby.

In June Anna and David went to Wurtemberg to visit his relatives and they also stayed at Heiden, a village in a beautiful setting overlooking Lake Constance. By September they were back in England making plans for their return to Ibadan.

Before leaving England in October they again visited their friends the Revd. Richard Hone and his family at Halesowen Rectory and were there on the 20th October, the last Sunday of their stay. Richard Hone reported how very much the Halesowen Church members were impressed with their eagerness and enthusiasm for returning to Ibadan in spite of the troubles of their last years there. Anna gave a brief farewell talk to the school children and specially asked them to do what St. Paul had requested the Christians at Corinth to do when he wrote a letter to them. She told them of the Bible verse which says, 'Ye also helping together by prayer for us.' (2 Corinthians 1:11 in the Authorized Version of the Bible.)

Leaving Halesowen they travelled to Liverpool and on 24th October set sail in the *S.S. Calabar,* arriving at Lagos on 19th November. From there they sent word to Ibadan telling them of their arrival, knowing that willing people would come to help as they had brought a large amount of much needed goods and equipment. That would have included the harmonium.

By this time the Governor of Lagos had negotiated with the Ijebu people a safe overland route to Ibadan and that was the track they took for several days, arriving just before Christmas to a rapturous welcome which Anna described in a letter dated December 29th: 'We had a very favoured voyage, and reached Lagos on the 19th. I had a good share of sea-sickness, but was not so thoroughly ill as before. It was very sweet to think of you all praying for us, and our gracious God heard and answered. We rested a short time there, and then prepared our things for the interior. About forty Ibadan people came to carry them for us. We slept one night at Ikorodu [on the north side of Lagos Lagoon] and then began our three days' land journey, which was very well accomplished, except that on the second day my husband had an attack of fever, and being worse the next day, was obliged to rest many times, which made us arrive late in Ibadan, to the disappointment of a great many.

All the church people had come out some miles on the road, and the children could not eat for excitement. Late as we were, some of them waited, and the shouts and screams, who can describe? As we neared our dwelling, the children burst forth in singing, "How beautiful upon the mountains;" and as we went up the steps of our house, they sang, "Welcome home." It was very pretty of them. Our house was filled for days. I had much to do, for our things had got wet, having been carried up in baskets.'

Then Anna described one horror of homecoming: 'In our absence, the white ants took a fancy to our bedroom, and I did not know it. One portmanteau had been covered with tarpaulin, so I knew that it could not be wet, and did not mean to open it for some time, but wanting something out of it, after three days I opened it, and oh, the dismay! You can hardly imagine the scene, my dresses were completely eaten through, and the linen also.' As their boxes no longer had the lead linings, which had been stripped out and sold when they were so desperately in need of cowries, the white ants had been able to eat nearly everything inside. However, that was a minor inconvenience compared with troubles to come.

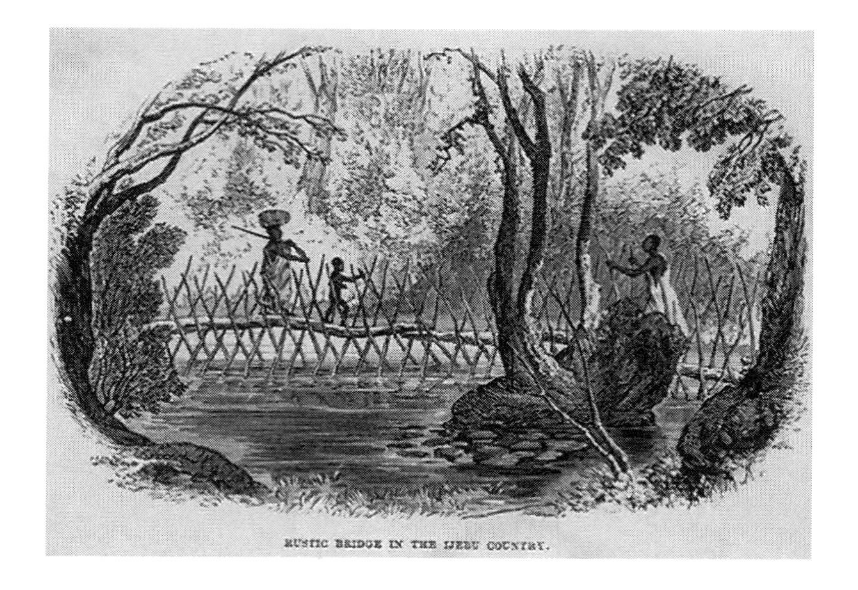

RUSTIC BRIDGE IN THE IJEBU COUNTRY.

# Chapter 8 The third stay in Ibadan 1866 to 1869

As it was just before Christmas 1866 when Anna and David finally reached home in Ibadan, they did not arrive in time to prepare for the usual Christmas festivities so those were deferred until 27th December when they had a special party for the school children and gave presents to them all.

## 1867

The traditional New Year's Day service was held on January 1st followed by a festive meal provided for all the people who attended but sadly Anna had developed the fever so often experienced soon after arriving in Africa. By the end of the month she was able to write again: 'January 30th: I am but slowly recovering from such a severe attack as I hardly ever experienced. People try to encourage me by saying, having had this, I may expect unusual health. It has been a great trial and disappointment to be so very ill, and still to remain so weak; there seems so much to be done, which only I can do. It was a great comfort to have my husband recovered before my illness began; his hands are more than full, with five classes in a week, beside services, but he is happy if only strength may be given.

I miss my Konigbagbe sadly; she has a little baby as good-tempered as herself, and she and her husband go on very well. Mrs. Olubi [Susanna] has her hands full with her four children and assisting me in the sewing-school. They are all delighted at having us back."

While Anna and David were away, the staff had been busily continuing the work of preaching and teaching new converts. To their great joy a service of Baptism was held soon after their return.

Life at the Mission is not so often mentioned in letters from David. However, on January 31st he wrote: 'My dear wife probably has mentioned the baptism of eighteen adults, three lads, and four children. Most of them have rejoiced my heart on examining them, especially a boy of about eight years of age, whom I wanted to wait till he was a little older, fearing that he was too young to make up his mind as to whom he would serve. But he went to his guardian, a relation of his, who redeemed him from slavery, and is himself a convert, saying, "You must take me to the white man, and beg for me, and tell him I am not too young to serve God; I will not serve the devil. Jesus I want to follow and I want to be baptized now." He told his grandmother of his intention and the poor old woman was very angry; whereupon he told her all he knew about Jesus, how He suffered and died for us. The woman was not to be moved. The boy burst out crying, and said, "How can it be possible for people to hear such good words and not to believe?" Who shall hinder that such should not be baptized? He was baptized by the name of Samuel, which he himself chose.'

As the following letter illustrates, there was a great deal of work to be done and the routine of the Mission was resumed as soon as possible with Anna's characteristic enthusiasm. On February 21st Anna wrote: 'Thank God, I am now getting into work again. Three of the boys are learning the harmonium; it is a work of patience, in a hot country, only to have to hear it. I have Akielle and Oyebode every morning for lessons, general history, geography, etc. … the girls for sewing from twelve to two o'clock, and I am now forming a class of women who live near us, to teach them to sew, once a week. These are some of the regular doings, and the irregular may be called legion; doctoring, mending, housekeeping, receiving visitors. Ogunyomi I use in the house; her temper is her great trial, but we get on, and she has love in her heart which helps through. I give her reading and writing lessons every evening, except Monday and Saturday, with two or three other girls. Olubi has been to Abeokuta, as his mother was in her dying illness. He had the satisfaction of attending and comforting her in her last days upon earth, and seeing her depart in peace, in full faith and trust in her Lord and Saviour.

Poor Arubo, they say, when he had seen the last of me, burst into floods of tears, and bye and bye exclaimed, "I shall never see Iya in Ibadan again;" but I think he did not expect us to return, on account of the great trials we had through the war. We have a good many growing up around us now, and we have many an anxiety concerning them. However, we must work on, waiting for fruit.'

'April 2nd: We have had such a month of awful sickness in the town, death in every house, small-pox quite a pestilence, and no rain. The heat is intense, it is a weariness to look day by day at the cloudless sky, but we had one shower the night before last, which, I trust, will do some good, yet we thirst for more. Two white head-ties, from Dawlish, adorned the heads of two young brides yesterday. Susanna Abayomi was one, the girl who minded my dear little Eyila, so well.'

During the April heat Bashorun, the head chief of the town, died and the resulting activities described by Anna were quite extraordinary. 'You might almost hear a pin drop to-day, the town is so quiet. It is the second burial for Bashorun. His horse is to be killed on his grave; no market is allowed. At twelve o'clock feasting is to begin, and thousands will go to it. They may steal and do as they like to-day without being punished, in honour of Bashorun. Such are their schemes to bury the thought of death; they eat, drink, and fire guns that death may not be what it really is after all - a fear and terror to them.'

'April 30th: The *Pilgrim's Progress* is becoming appreciated by our people. My class of women on Sunday afternoons are greedy for it. We each read a paragraph, and talk about it; and on the Sunday evenings, after a little Scripture-repeating and hymn-singing, I read it with my girls, and D. with the boys; they are perfectly charmed.

Ogunyomi is suffering fearfully from a whitlow. She said if we could always read *Pilgrim* she might forget the pain. Their open mouths and exclamations, when the full meaning of something in it presents itself vividly before them, are most entertaining.

Many are preparing their money to buy it, and then it will go to farms and houses, and be quite the family book, but it is a little expensive for them; three shillings, or four thousand cowries! and food is very dear, from a scarcity of rain last year, and none yet this year. All the newly-planted corn is dried up, and the yams in a poor condition.'

Every June the Yoruba people celebrated the feast of the Egungun - spirits of the ancestors - by holding masquerades and feasting. 'June 20th: "Our whole town is in an uproar, for seven days making the annual feast for Egungun, so-called spirits from the other world. The eating and drinking, dancing, and drumming, are awful. Next will come the worship of the god of the farms, when all will eat new yams; after which we have peaceful nights again for months.

In the midst of all this noise and confusion, these dark and evil doings, our dear Lucy Fagbeade, Ogunyomi's mother, fell asleep in Jesus. She was a very sincere woman, who extremely disliked much talking and noise about things in religion ... and in suffering, a few verses from God's Book always comforted and soothed her. Eleven years ago we redeemed her from slavery, when she was apparently sick unto death, that her child might nurse her, and soothe her dying hours; and God has spared her eleven years, and redeemed her soul by the precious blood of Christ, and has now taken her to dwell with Him for ever. God be praised! She lived in the compound, became cook for the children, and was always useful, cheerful, happy, and thankful. Ogunyomi feels her mother's death; they were so much attached to one another; but all the mercies shown to her, her simple Christian life after so many years of dark heathen practices, and her happy death, soften her mourning, and make her happy in the midst of all.

I have little Bertha Olubi to live with me for the present. I like a little child about the house, it is so cheerful, and she is happy enough and troublesome enough too sometimes. I always think that the trouble of a child is rather good for my nature and disposition. Her little woolly head is the most difficult to keep neat. Their heads, when their mothers cannot do them, are done by regular hairplaiters in the town, which has to last some weeks without being undone; which plan I do not approve, so I make my girls plait their hair once a week. I do Bertha's after a fashion of my own. You must use a great wooden comb, and drag it through the hair straight upwards! Then I part it down the middle, and three or four places on each side, and then take each little tuft, and drag and plait it as tight as possible, and it hangs down in many short little plaited tails. It would hurt you and me, but their hard heads are used to it, and Bertha often falls asleep while I am doing it!

Many strangers come to church on Sunday, to see if it is true that many of their townspeople have joined the Christian religion. A few Sundays ago seven persons were baptized. In one we were particularly interested; a blacksmith, who seems to have partaken of the true change, and on whom the Spirit of Life has breathed. Okusehinde, one of our scripture readers, was the means of bringing him into the blessed fold. We have ninety-six communicants; at our last, eighty-eight were present, and those absent were ill, or in other towns. So we have much to make us hope, but we are longing to see new ones coming forward to enlist on the Lord's side.'

The following is an account of a typical Sunday in Ibadan, written about this time by Anna for the *Church Missionary School Magazine.*

'Though our house and church are surrounded by heathen neighbours, some friendly to us, and some not, I always feel there is a good deal of respect shown to us and our day, by these same heathen people. We are very rarely annoyed by any one coming to offer anything to sell on that day; there is far less noise around us than on other days.

Some very near to us have given up, of their own accord, using their cloth-dyeing establishments, and little markets, going to other occupations further off, and this not from any request on our part, for we did not feel we had the least right to ask it of them. Our quiet orderly services seem of themselves to procure respect so different from anything of their own, whether heathen or Mohammedan.

Our church is very simple, but quite neat, 70 feet by 30, its hard, stony, mud walls straight and smooth, coloured with a pale red wash; containing benches fastened in the ground, neat communion-table, rails, and pulpit, cut and manufactured by Africans, under our superintendence. We also moulded a very pretty font, forming it as well and as neatly as we could with wet clay; we painted it white.

How very cheering is the sound of our first bell, at half-past eight on Sunday morning, rung so cheerfully and heartily by one of our little African boys! The bell is on the outside of the church at one end, with a neat little roof of boards over it, to protect it from the hot sun and heavy rains; this also takes off the barn-like look our church might otherwise have from its thatched roof. We have plenty of air and light, many windows without glass, the shutters always open, only closed at night and in heavy rains. A heavy tornado does trouble us sometimes; the storm is so furious that prayer or preaching has to cease for about a quarter of an hour, as there would be no possibility of a word being heard.

The first bell rings at half-past eight: from then till a few minutes before nine, when the second bell rings, we can look out and see our people coming, with their nice English bags of coloured print, or their own grass bags, on their heads, containing their books; some with only the Primer, others, more advanced in the new art of reading, with various portions of the Word of God; St. Luke, the Psalms, Proverbs, and Genesis, being among the great favourites. Now the whole of the New Testament is complete, and bound in one volume, and our people will, I know, be much delighted with such a volume.

We see the people hastening towards us as nine o'clock approaches, for the one hour for school is too precious to be wasted by being five minutes too late. The school consists of men and women, who are most anxiously and diligently reading, and learning to read; men on one side the church, and women on the other. We have to use our more advanced day-scholars as teachers for some classes, and it is very pretty to see the thankfulness and attention of these men and women, some with grey hairs, to their young teachers, and they often bring them presents of honey or fruit, to tempt these children to go on teaching them when the school is over.

We have about eight or nine classes of different stages; and a very interesting assembly, at the bottom of the church, of those who cannot learn to read. We gather these together and first tell them a short simple Bible story, and let them tell it us again, to see that they remember it, and take it in. Then we teach them a text, or a verse of a hymn, and the last quarter of an hour is always given in all the classes to teaching by repetition some catechism, and sometimes for change we have the whole school together to go over the Creed, the Lord's Prayer, and the Ten Commandments, to make sure they are not forgotten. Oh, what bright, eager, earnest, black, shining faces we have in our African Sunday school!

At ten o clock we have to leave off, to give them opportunity to make ready for service at half-past ten; for the babies come as well as the mothers, and they are allowed the freedom of creeping about, or being nursed by others not much bigger than themselves, during school-time; but for church they must be packed on their mothers backs to go to sleep. In that half hour, many of the women and most of the men gather in groups, talking over what they have been reading, or making enquiries and remarks on some things which have struck them in their reading by themselves in their own houses, in the course of the week.

YORUBA MOTHER AND CHILD.

At half-past ten, service commences; our singing is hearty, our responses very hearty, and the attention to the sermon is also gratifying. We are out by twelve. Our town being so large, many members of our congregation come a distance of between two or three miles; so they bring their dinners with them, spread their mats in our verandahs, take their meal and a little sleep, and a great deal of conversation. At three precisely we meet again for an hour's school, the proceedings much the same as in the morning, except that the last quarter of an hour is generally given to questioning them on the sermon, which shakes up their attention, and always gives us opportunity of explaining some things more particularly. This is followed by service, and all is over by half past five, when everybody hurries to get back to their houses before dark, as it is always dark by a quarter-past six.

We have often many heathen visitors; some attracted by the sound of the bell, which they may notice for the first time; others by our hymn-singing, or chanting, which causes them to wonder what is going on inside that large and straight building. A person enters, and finds the white man speaking or praying, and does not take immediate hold of that, feeling it is sure to be in an unknown tongue, as among the Mohammedans; so he amuses himself with looking at the people, then the roof, the smooth straight wall, the benches, the windows, till bye and bye, all at once, he finds the sounds that have been falling on his ear are in his own native tongue; then come the fixed attention, the open mouth, the gazing eye; and different sentences from our beautiful church service find acceptance in his wondering mind; the hands are rubbed as a sign of approbation, with a quiet expression of it in the word "emo! – wonderful!"

When all sorts and conditions of people are prayed for, the kindly fruits of the earth in their season asked for, and so on, he sometimes cannot wait for the response, and does not know that one is to come, but bursts forth with his own hearty "Amin, Amin!" clapping his hands and his chest; and then perhaps goes away to talk with his heathen companions over what he had heard, and to commend the religion of the white man; wondering greatly at much that he has heard, especially at our praying for our enemies.

Our evening is spent by the children gathering round us, to whom we can hardly give any attention in the day. They repeat passages of Scripture learned by heart from us, and we sing English and Yoruba hymns, to sweet English tunes, with the harmonium.

Blessed, happy Sundays! Wearied and tired we often are, and very glad, when the day is done, to lay our poor bodies down to rest in the sweet thought –

"Yet shall there dawn at last a day,
A sun that never sets shall rise,
Night shall not veil its ceaseless ray,
The heavenly Sabbath never dies!"

And there and then shall be gathered a blessed assembly from among all nations, and peoples, and tongues.'

It is quite amazing to realize how many people lived in the Mission compound, making it the home of an enormously extended family.

'July 23rd: We have nothing of particular interest to communicate this month, except that Antonio has been called to the kingdom above. "I am going to Jesus, who lived and died for me" were nearly his last words. He was an emigrant from the Brazils, where he had been carried as a slave, and, on coming back to this country, did not get on with his relations, who treated him very badly; so ten years ago he begged us to let him lodge in a little room in our compound for a few weeks, which came to ten years, though he lived principally on his farm. Living in our compound, he always attended church and from one and another, the good tidings of salvation were set before him. At length the seed sown sank down into his heart, and he became a changed man.

He felt himself too old to learn to read Yoruba, and I did not know, till I was leaving for England, that he could read Portuguese; but he never had any book but the Romish calendar of saints. We sent him a Bible, which has been the greatest pleasure to him; he feasted on the reading of it, and longed to teach me Portuguese, that we might talk about it; but then came his wife's illness, then my illness, then his own, so we shall never talk Portuguese, but we shall be able to speak the language of Canaan, when we meet in that land where there is no more death. His nice wife died on New Year's Day, with the name of Jesus on her dying lips. So heaven's gates are opened to take in some of these poor souls, long living in heathen darkness and in Satan's chains, for whom we pray and labour, and for whom Christ has died. To Him be all honour and glory.

I have now his two orphans, his eldest girl Talabi, who has lived with me these ten years, and the little babe of two years, who was given to me by his mother, begging me to nurse him for her. The day she died, some of the heathen relations gave us great trouble; they wanted to get the children, just to become slaves to them, but with quite a battle we maintained our right to them, and

God gave us the victory. But this girl is a wonderful trouble … and I have much anxiety, now that she is growing up.

Little Samuel [who was baptized earlier in the year] is going on very nicely, and goes to our second day-school. For a time his mother was in the compound in which he resides, but he has been greatly grieved that she has left it to dwell among the heathen. He cried much, because he hoped she would hear the Word of God; but now, he says, she throws salvation away from her.'

'August 14th: His mother is now redeemed, and has every opportunity of coming to church, but she stoutly refuses, and says her father's gods are quite enough for her. But the little fellow told me last Sunday evening, with a feeling of hope, "Though my mother will not come herself, she says she will not prevent me; that is good, is it not?"'

The last few months of 1867 were anxious ones as the whole Yoruba country became unsettled again through tribal warfare and hostility against the European Christians. The churches at Abeokuta were attacked and destroyed and the missionaries there had to flee to Lagos for their lives. Would the heathen people of Ibadan behave in the same way? Would the chiefs of Ibadan wish to expel the missionaries from their town too? David had earnest discussion with the chiefs about the situation and was greatly relieved by their words of assurance: "We have let you do your work, and we have done ours, but you little know how closely we have watched you and your ways please us. We have not only looked at your mouths but at your hands, and we have no complaint to lay against you. Just go on with your work with a quiet mind; you are our friends, and we are yours."

The Egba and Ijebu tribes were not pleased with the decision of the Ibadan chiefs to allow the missionaries to stay and they therefore closed the route to the coast again, making it difficult for letters and supplies to be transported and all the former difficulties of communication arose again. Undoubtedly increasing anxieties and the season of hot weather probably contributed to the ill health of Anna and David.

A letter of November 19th from Anna explained: 'My dear husband has lately had a sharp attack of fever, which is general at the commencement of the hot season; which trying season we have now to look for, through the next six months; but perhaps, before the end of that time, we may, through mercy and love, have reached the rest where storms shall never burst, suns shall never smite, and the inhabitant shall no more say, I am sick. The weight upon us is sometimes very great, and but for the sustaining Hand we must sink.'

David and Anna's intention always was to make the Christians of Ibadan aware that they were members of a universal church, that there were Christians in other parts of the world and that they all needed to pray for each other and contribute to their own churches and when necessary to the needs of others. Therefore they were greatly cheered in November by the response to an appeal they had made several months before.

Anna's letter of November 30th told with considerable gratification: 'We have had a very busy week collecting cowries. Since our return we have been trying to teach our people to give. Every month we have a prayer meeting, and now every third month we have united with it a kind of missionary meeting, to give the people an account of the work of God in other lands, and we have advised them to have large pots, with small mouths, in which to put their odd money any day, and once a week to put in it something special. This has been the week to gather them in. Some of them have done exceedingly well and entered heartily into the plan, especially the children who have jumped at many devices for making cowries to drop into the "Apo Oluwa." Some have not made much effort, but altogether we are much pleased, considering there is not a rich person among them, that we shall have more than thirty bags of cowries to offer to the Church Missionary Society. As each bag contains 20,000 cowry shells, you may think my business has not been small.'

The collection of cowries totalled the amazing sum of £20 5s.7d. This does not sound very much to us today, but it was extremely sacrificial giving for those concerned at that time.

## 1868

The beginning of 1868 was a time for much deliberation over the future of the church in Ibadan. David and Anna became increasingly aware that because of their own health problems, combined with the vagaries of the climate, their days of service in Africa could not continue for very much longer. The unsettled local situation made it unlikely that other European missionaries would be permitted to live at Ibadan in the foreseeable future. Therefore the future of the Mission must depend on the African Christians in whom they had always invested a great deal of their time in teaching. David felt that those whom he had trained as catechists should be prepared for ordination and that there were younger members of the church who would with training become excellent teachers to follow in their footsteps.

By this time the first church at Kudeti had more than one hundred baptized members and many others who regularly attended but had not yet made any firm Christian commitment. In addition there were two other 'daughter' Missions in other parts of Ibadan. At Oke Aremo there was a temporary church with ninety members as well as numerous interested attenders. There was another church at Oke Ogunpa about two miles away from Kudeti which had been established for over eight years but was not so flourishing. It was under the care of William Allen, one of the catechists who had been recruited from Sierra Leone. He had become somewhat disheartened. What should be done about that situation? Would a new approach stir up the people there and revitalize that little struggling church? It was eventually decided that William Allen and Daniel Olubi should exchange their positions.

For Daniel Olubi this was going to be a tremendous challenge which he knew he must rise to. His reaction was published in the *Church Missionary Record* of 1869 as follows: 'On removing to this station, though it is in Ibadan, and only two miles from my former home in Kudeti, I must remark it has been a great pain to myself, my wife and children, to go from under the roof of our dear master and mistress. For near nineteen years I have lived in one capacity or other with the Rev. D. Hinderer; and my wife, before I married her, lived with Mrs. Hinderer ever since she came out in 1852, and we have indeed found them not only kind and good, and a faithful master and mistress, but a true father and mother and friends. So no wonder we all feel this parting; but it is for our Master's service. May God long preserve them!'

Anna also felt a great loss at this turn of events. She wrote: 'January 25th 1868: We are going to lose Olubi; which is a trial; we are so used to him. His wife has been with me more than fifteen years, and their children have been my great pleasure. We are placing him in the third station, about two miles from us, in the north-west part of the town, where Mr. Jeffries died, and Mr. Roper lived in hard times.'

The hot season in the early months of 1868 was bearable but then Anna developed a cough which was with her for many weeks and much wearied her. Although her faith never faltered, nor did her enthusiasm for her work diminish, there were signs that Anna was having increasing difficulty in mustering the energy required to carry out her duties.

'April 21st: In our work we are going on with some measure of discouragement, crosses, and toil, but a bright side too is given, one of hope and encouragement; and we feel that the Lord is owning and blessing His work…

I have so much to do at home I never go beyond the compound, except to sick people, unless I am quite obliged. I feel that going out knocks me down more than anything. Some of my girls have married, and some of our boys, after many years of labour for them, have gone after their own ways and pleasures; so there are not so many in and about the house; only seven girls and five boys in the house and eight in the compound, but we have about thirty-six in our day-school, and at our second station thirty-eight and all have to be attended to and cared for, in divers ways.

My husband's health is far from good, and some times we have feared a thorough break-up; then renewed strength comes again, and he is so quietly persevering, that he gets through a great deal. He is much interested in instructing the native teachers and two or three boys, who have grown up with us within the last fifteen years, and who bid fair to be very useful members of society; of course they came out of heathen households, and it is a great happiness to see them turning out well. We have been favoured to bring up some to do God's work in their own country, which has ever been an aim and object with us. God gives us such comfort in our native teachers, they are so earnest, kind, and affectionate to us, only desiring to relieve, help, and comfort us.'

'May 14th: The seed of the kingdom is being largely sown at this time, in this huge mass of heathen darkness, in various ways. A few of the older members of the Church are quietly, but truly and earnestly, bearing witness among heathen relations, friends, and neighbours. Little Samuel has been very ill; I often felt he would go, and dared not ask for his life.'

David Hinderer wrote about this time: 'We have the comfort of seeing some of our native teachers promise to become efficient ministers of the Gospel, and foremost among them is Daniel Olubi. He seems to be increasingly faithful, diligent and pious, and I hope, ere long, he will be ordained by Bishop Crowther. He was nearly overcome at the thought, when I mentioned my intention of recommending him for ordination: the weight of the responsibility, and the thought of his insufficiency lie heavily upon him.'

In 1864 their friend, the Reverend Samuel Crowther, had been consecrated Bishop of 'The Countries of Western Africa beyond the limits of the Queen's dominions.' He was the first African Bishop.

Bishop Samuel Ajayi Crowther

Anna's next letter was dated July 30th: 'Mr. Hinderer has been suffering from congestion of the lungs, which gave him often a severe and cramp-like pain in the heart; he is better, but never well, and is never out of pain. We have many weights on our hearts about the mission, but the Lord sitteth above the water-flood.'

'September 12th: With a weak and suffering body, D. is getting up a nice church in Aremo, our second station, and a more simple one is now completed in Ogunpa, the third station, where Olubi is. I have been very ill the last six weeks, and have spent all but four or five days of them in much fever and suffering. Now that I am creeping up the hill, I should be glad of many little things to help me, which I should have, if the road were open, but I am getting on without them, and it is almost more trial to my ever kind husband, to be unable to get for me these helps and comforts. Our prospects are no better. We cannot help often fearing we shall break down, before better and more peaceful times come.

Last Sunday I was up, but could not go out; many passages in Job were helpful to my spirit: "He openeth their ear to discipline…" Too often we 'see not the bright light' in the clouds, and are much cast down and discouraged. Truly, the future is very dark, but in the midst of all, we may be sure, the bright light is in the cloud and it must be for our Master's good purpose, that He has placed and keeps us here so long.'

'October 23rd: I am now much better, but recovery seems sadly slow. I am a good deal worn out in body and spirit, and probably I shall never be strong again. I am so tender, can only sit with pillows round me, and just crawl from one room to another and I am dreading the thought of the heat, which must soon come, but sufficient unto the day is the evil thereof. "Give us this day our daily bread." We are not told to ask for tomorrow's bread. My husband is quite wonderful. After all his care and anxiety for me, I feared for him, but now he is so much better than for months before. Oh, how the Father stays the rough wind in the day of the east wind!

We have had such trial in two of our big boys turning out so wickedly, full of charms and poisons, and determined to do everything with the heathen. Many thorns are in the pillow, but there is another pillow on which to lean the aching heart and head. What should we do without that?

As to the work, we try to be hopeful, but it is far below what we want it to be. There is some movement. The heathen talk about the Christian's religion, they ask questions far more than they used to do, and listen to the teaching in the streets, and often drop into church. In a remarkable manner, some, on their dying beds, have borne witness to the faithful teaching, and have shown that they believed its truth, and regretted that they had shut their ears to it. About a fortnight ago, a man died: he had only been once to church, but Olubi and Okusehinde had often visited him, and he had heard them in the streets. He was interested, but said it was impossible for such as him to follow our way, yet he could never get it out of his mind; and then he fell ill and sent for my husband. It was the first time a heathen man had sent for him. He was very weak, but his conversation was such as gives joy to the heart. He anxiously enquired if there was any help for him, now life was ending, since he had displeased God all his days. After some conversation and prayer, he seemed to have a bright glimmer of hope and folding his hands, said, "May God have mercy and if there is such a Saviour as the white man says there is, may He help me." When they saw him again he could not speak, but put his hands together and lifted them up. Two days after he died.

We think that He who took the dying thief in His arms of love and mercy did not turn away from this poor man. Such gleams of hope coming, though rare are a wonderful help over the many dark and rough places!'

'October 26th: Only last Thursday we received the March mail. An Ijebu man, who has a house in Ibadan, assured the governor he was coming here direct, so he gave him that mail to bring to us. … He stayed six months in Ijebu, but tells us, he took such good care of the parcel, he slept on it every night, that no one should take it away.

I am getting on but slowly, and do not feel so well to-day. I think I am no more what I have been; my rather remarkable rallying power after an illness seems gone; still I may get round again. We have just had such a storm of wind and rain, which has spoiled all my lovely orange-blossoms. [Was this from a tree grown from the seed given to Anna by the old man in Sierra Leone?] The trees have been such a pleasant sight, with an abundance of ripe fruit, though we have gathered, and given away baskets full; at the same time, all the ends of the branches have been so rich in bright fresh young leaves, and those elegant sweet-smelling blossoms; but now the beauty has gone within half an hour. It is so with things of earth; but after this comes the new fruit.'

'November 30th: On Advent Sunday eight adults were admitted, by baptism, into the visible church. One was a very old man, one of the royal family now settled in Oyo, formerly Katunga, which Mungo Park and other travellers visited in its glory. This old man saw all these travellers. He was an heir to the throne, and his name Adeyemi, signifies, 'a crown fits me,' but the earthly crown had indeed failed him. Among the different wars, he has been taken captive by three different tribes, and has undergone many hardships. Five years ago, being old, and nearly useless, he redeemed himself for a few bags of cowries, and reached Ibadan, where he practised his great medicine and charm knowledge. He found a sister here, who gave him a room in her compound; but, when he was very ill, she put him out in the street to die, as it would be impossible for her to bury one who had been heir to a crown. The poor old man dwelt under a tree, and struggled through his illness and the passers-by, knowing or learning who he was, gave him cowries, or a little food. One of our young schoolmasters who, sixteen years ago was one of the first African children we took into our house, became much interested in him and, while administering to his bodily needs, would talk to him about his soul. But the old man was greatly enraged, and heaped curses on the youth for daring to speak to him of a way better than his own, stoutly defending the worship of his idols, and only wishing to go to the heaven where they would take him. To the surprise of all, he recovered. Another relation took him in, and our schoolmaster still visited him. At last light broke in upon his poor dark mind, and he now seems to be rejoicing in his Saviour and the prospect before him.

On the day of their baptism, the candidates had been sitting on the front benches in the church, in their white garments, and, as they walked down the aisle to the font, we all sang a hymn, which my husband had composed in Yoruba, on "Be thou faithful" to the tune we call *Halesowen*. It was very touching to see the old man at the font, leaning on his long staff, as we might imagine Jacob to have done before Pharaoh, his lips quivering with old age, and his eyes gleaming with pleasure and perfect child-like belief and trust, making the responses, of which he certainly put in some which were not in the book.

The others have a history more or less interesting, which gives us every reason to believe that they have laid hold of the hope set before them. This is the bright side of our life in this country, and often such a time has cheered and comforted us, while passing through many storms and waves. We feel as if we could never give up until we cross to the other side of the river.

We cannot tell you now the darker side of our life, its present and prospective difficulties. It is the burden appointed us to carry, and we shall not be left alone to bear it; yet we do feel it heavy, and often groan under it. But the day hasteth on, the shadows of evening are stretched out, and oh, if infinite mercy and love receive us, we shall then think the heaviest weight, care, and sorrow to have been but light indeed. I am not in a good state of health, and my spirits have undergone such a change; I believe the latter is but the effect of the former. A thorough change would be the best remedy; but when the 'grasshopper is a burden,' the body shrinks from a four days journey, in this broiling sun, to the coast; yet I dare say it will be accomplished, and in some measure I am making ready for it, putting things to rights, and getting to the end of some of our lesson-books with the boys.

I think I told you I had little Bertha Olubi back. I thought a child might rouse me a little. Her little sister Tilda grows so nicely, and is so entertaining. She and her mother came to stay a day or two with me. The child, seeing me not so lively as usual, threw herself on my lap one evening, and said, in Yoruba of course, "Iya, do laugh" and then made up the most ridiculous little grinning face, to show me how to laugh, which had its full effect; and then she danced, and clapped her hands, singing, "I have made Iya laugh! I have made Iya laugh!"

These letters of 1868 reveal how Anna and David are showing increasing signs of stress and strain. They are carrying a burden which is weighing very heavily but which they are bearing with great fortitude. At Christmas time Anna hoped that she might go to Lagos for a break and medical treatment. However, they heard that there was a plot against her life if she decided to set out on the journey.

A strange messenger arrived at the Mission on New Year's Eve. Captain Glover, ever mindful of the plight of the missionaries, had sent him with instruction to return to the coast with Anna and David. They had been in this situation before! Again David knew that he could just not walk away from his responsibilities. For Anna, it was different. Her health was giving such grave cause for concern that they realized that she must take the opportunity to make the journey to Lagos but if she had gone straight away the New Year festivities would have been ruined. Having made elaborate preparations for them she was determined to stay long enough to carry them out.

## 1869

The traditional New Years' Day service was held at Oke Ogunpa to celebrate the opening of the new church there – one of the daughter churches to Kudeti about two miles away. A church had been built on a hill there for the congregation of about one hundred who had formerly attended Kudeti Church. 'They used to come to us, and bring their dinner. After a while we made a large shed in that quarter and gave them a service in the afternoon. Now, for many reasons, we felt it was time they should have a separate church. Some of them were getting into years, and felt it burdensome to come so far to church; and we also felt that having a church there would be a fresh inducement to try and draw others in.

All the three congregations assembled at the new church, and they had a cheering and refreshing service. Afterwards some three hundred persons partook of a feast which we make for them every year; having had the children a few days before. It was a very happy day. I had been so busy all the week before, buying things for it, and was up there the whole of the previous day, superintending the preparation. Oh, I was tired, but my spirits can carry me through much fatigue. Laniyono and Konigbagbe are the schoolmaster and mistress there and they did work. Koni is so energetic; she had my best powers spent on her, and she is capital. Laniyono is doing well, persevering and industrious. Olubi is working on hard ground, and is first-rate. I have groaned and grudged giving him up, but it was right; only we both lost a right hand.

I kept the messenger a few days, to make ready again; and by moonlight one morning, [January 5th] before the plotters would be awake, we set off. We came as fast as possible; I was not allowed to put my foot into a house. We slept in the bush; found the Governor's boat, which had been waiting some days in expectation; went rapidly over the lagoon, and in the evening of the third day we landed in Lagos and I was once more a free woman! Little Dan Olubi is with me, bright and sharp as a needle; Oyebode I have also brought, to learn something of printing, that we may be able to make use of our press. I can send them home by Abeokuta any day, as that road is open to all but white people.'

'Lagos, January 25th: I must write when I can, to be ready for the mail, which seems to come and go in a marvellously short space of time. I cannot yet recover myself, my daily life upset; such a separation from my husband; I cannot hear from him, nor send to him, as I should like; but I am thankful to have been able to send him, by my carriers, some of the necessaries, if not the comforts, of life. Here there is so much coming and going, I feel bewildered, and do not get settled; and as to my health, I have made no progress as yet. The doctor says I have had a thorough shock to the constitution; that I am one of a hundred to be in the country at all, and that I must go home. I wish I could have a clear direction, as Moses had, "Ye have dwelt long enough in this mount; turn you, and take your journey and go." On the whole, we have had a rough path in our missionary life, but it has been always brightened by hope. We have been mercifully helped through difficult places, and marvellously favoured to carry music in the heart. The darkest day has always had sunshine in it, and at this moment, in Ibadan, there is much cause for hope in many ways. Never were chiefs and people more kind to us in their way; never were we more respected than now; and never did people more patiently listen to teaching, though we do not see the fruit of it as much as we should like.

When we look at what is wanted and desired, we may say, what is the result? But on the whole, we have been permitted to see much that makes our hearts glad and thankful. We came to a town where the name of Jesus had never been heard; that name, and the salvation which He gives, have been proclaimed through the length and breadth of it; many are thinking and talking of it; a small company have believed and rejoiced in that name and have died in faith, and trust, and hope; others are walking in the light of it, and others taking first steps in the Christian life. To leave it all is such a sorrow to our hearts, that if we had even bodily strength it must tell upon us. May our God graciously direct our steps! In all probability I shall have to go to England in two or three months, but indeed the to-morrow is very dark. I do not like leaving my husband alone, but we agreed, before parting, to yield to what seems right and best, trusting to be directed by our heavenly Father.'

Shortly after that letter was sent, Anna had an exceptionally severe attack of sickness, making it imperative that she should seek medical attention in England. As a ship was due to leave she hurriedly wrote a letter on February 3rd saying: 'There is a mail leaving to-morrow, so I just add a line. I have been very ill, and the doctor and others have wanted to send me off by it; but as I am better, I have pleaded to remain till this time next month that I may send to and hear from my dear husband. He will be quite prepared for the decision. I have just parted with my two boys Dan and Oyebode; it is better to have them back at their own place; but we have had a sorrowful parting, they cried bitterly. . .

I hope we shall meet before long, but oh, these present moments are rough and thorny, many are the pangs. God comfort, help, lead, and direct. It is so sad to feel I shall never see poor dear Ibadan again, and all my babies. Well, well, there is a land above, no seas there shall sever. You will feel and care for me in the heavy trial of leaving my husband behind, and going home alone.'

By the same mail she wrote to another friend: 'Our people's and children's letters are most piteous. It has been the mission and work of our hearts. Pray for poor lonely me, as I shall be on my voyage when you get this letter; and for my dear husband. … Pray for poor Ibadan, and the little 'garden' there.'

Sadly, about this time Laniyono was dismissed from the school at Oke Ogunpa for a misdemeanor which brought dishonour to the Christian work. Anna and David had nurtured him from a very early age, felt he had great promise and had put great trust in him. Therefore their disappointment was extremely acute. However, inappropriate behaviour of any sort could not be tolerated and they had to be very strict about that.

But there were success stories too. Akielle, the first scholar at their Mission school was appointed to be the master of the Kudeti school. Soon after that he and Ogunyomi were married and she became a wonderful helper in the work. Oyebode, to whom Anna had given special lessons with Akielle, was appointed to be the master at the school at Aremo.

When Anna embarked on the daunting lonely voyage to England on 7th March she at least knew that some of their labours were bearing good fruit.

# Chapter 9 Return to England and the final year of Anna's life

With favourable winds the voyage to England took fewer days than expected, yet an extremely travel-worn Anna disembarked from the *S.S. Mandingo* that docked at Liverpool on 1st April 1869 with 27 other passengers. News of her impending arrival would have reached England with the letters carried on the previous ship. Therefore no doubt it had been arranged that she would be met by Mr. and Mrs. Mather who lived at Bootle Hall not very far away.

They willingly took her home to stay with them for several days while she recovered from the voyage. From their house she wrote to David on April 7th: 'How I wish you could at this moment know how kindly and tenderly I am housed and sheltered in this home of love and comfort. We had a favoured journey over the mighty deep, and reached Liverpool on April 1st, four or five days before the time, though we had very rough seas and contrary winds, but mercifully no gale, of which there have been so many. I got on wonderfully, and was never so kindly treated. I was nursed and cared for as if I had been a child. ... I look forward to recovering now I am at home, but I have had much of illness since we parted in Ibadan; it was a struggle only to get sufficiently better at Lagos to bear the voyage.

These dear people, Mr. and Mrs. M., took no end of trouble to get me from the ship. ... In putting myself and boxes to rights, I got so ill that at times it was a question with me whether I should not suddenly depart. I was thankful when they brought their carriage and took me off; and I have had every luxury and comfort. If I had been as ill in Ibadan as I have been since I left it, I do not think I should be alive; so we must be thankful I got away when I did. Now, if I have rest and care and kindness, all of which I may expect, I think in time I shall be all right again; people are only ready to do too much for me. Fancy poor me, knocking about in the bush the other day, and now not allowed to take a first class railway journey without an attendant, and all sorts of luxuries!'

The next day Anna travelled by train to Halesowen to stay for several weeks with the Hone family at the Rectory there. They had become very valued friends whose hospitality she and David had greatly enjoyed during previous furloughs in England. With them she felt truly 'at home' and could relax and benefit as much as possible from the expert nursing care she received during severe bouts of pain and suffering.

It was probably a valuable time of de-briefing as she spent many hours telling them animatedly about the details of the last years at Ibadan and sometimes this left her utterly exhausted again. In spite of the state of her health it was evident that she still longed to return to Ibadan one day to continue the work there. However the Hone family realized that it was a forlorn hope. They wondered at times whether she would survive until she could be re-united with David.

Eventually Anna revived enough to contemplate another railway journey as she wished to visit friends (George Head Head and his wife Sarah née Gurney – a niece of Richenda Cunningham) at Rickerby House near Carlisle. There she was nursed through further illness but greatly enjoyed the beauty of their garden with the rhododendrons in full bloom and the distant view of green parkland beyond.

Being determined to visit as many friends as possible, she then travelled to Lowestoft via London. At Lowestoft she spent much time on the beach enjoying the sea breezes and felt much strengthened. One very elderly friend she visited did not at first recognize her even though she had known her since childhood. She was eventually convinced and absolutely overwhelmed with emotion, and then, when she had recovered, being a plain-spoken woman, she said 'Well dear, I am Mary still, and I don't hold to deceiving anybody, but my opinion is, dear, that you are booked, and not long for this world.' Anna's reply was that she hoped she was booked 'in the better land, but that she fancied she would have to wait a little longer before being called to dwell there.'

Often Anna watched for the mail to arrive in the hope that there was news from David but it was September before Anna heard that he had reached Lagos. Happily by the end of the month they were reunited in London.

During his last months in Ibadan David had suffered frequently from severe bouts of fever, giving those at the Mission extreme concern. David's main worry was that, knowing that no European would be permitted to continue his work, the Mission should continue in safe hands. He had tremendous confidence in the leadership of three of the African men who were well respected and trusted by the Christian converts as well as their heathen countrymen and who were truly united in bonds of brotherly love and affection for each other. He did hope to be present at the ordination of two of them, but that was not to be. To his great satisfaction though, before he left, the church at Aremo – the second mission in another part of Ibadan - was completed. Also, and vitally important, the Ibadan chiefs had promised that the Christian leaders and the Christian congregations would have their protection. It was not until Advent Sunday, 1871, that Daniel Olubi was ordained a Deacon at Lagos, by the Right Reverend Henry Cheetham who became the Bishop of Sierra Leone in 1870.

Anna and David stayed in London for several weeks to visit physicians and an oculist. Anna was having serious eye problems and unfortunately lost the sight in her right eye. The oculist thought that it was due to the African climate and that if she had remained there she would have gone blind. Only when she shut her eyes was she completely out of pain. Having received medical treatment they went to Norwich, staying for a few weeks of recommended rest but the time proved to be quite busy.

A friend writing later said 'I remember her, in her last visit to Norwich. She was there with Mr. Hinderer three months, shattered, yet still so bright. I saw much of her at that time; the same characteristics were there, faith, earnestness, brightness, cheerfulness, unselfishness. She told African tales to factory girls, spoke of dangers and toils and triumphs to listeners at a mothers' meeting; took snapdragon to the patients in a convalescent home; on Christmas eve distributed gifts from a Christmas tree to old and young; paid visits, and cheered many. Yet she was fading. …'

In January, Anna wrote: 'I do long that it may please God to show us soon what we ought to do, and direct us to a dwelling-place… So I hope we shall soon get into regular work, just enough for us half-worn-out pilgrims to do.'

Earlham Hall – now the Law School of the University of East Anglia

Surely their plight must have been widely talked about in the ecclesiastical circles of Norwich. David had taken part in a few services and they had both been speaking at various meetings. By this time their friend, the Reverend William Ripley, was vicar at St. Giles Church in the centre of Norwich. He had also married Laura, the young widow of John Gurney of Earlham Hall, who had several children. William and Laura and their still growing band of lively children continued to live there as it was such an ideally spacious home. It seems very likely that Anna and David stayed with the Ripley family at Earlham Hall.

Laura had grown up in Norwich Cathedral Close where her father the Reverend George Pearse was a Minor Canon. Later he had moved to a parish deep in the remote 'Island' of Flegg in east Norfolk. Now he was an elderly man in his 70s and in failing health. His wife had died and he sometimes stayed with William and Laura at Earlham Hall leaving his parish in the care of an assistant curate. He was at that time in need of help and was pleased to agree to a curacy for David together with the use of his Vicarage at Martham. As this offered Anna and David the home and the occupation they both desired they were absolutely delighted.

Before taking up residence in Martham, Anna and David stayed for a few days at Halesown Rectory with their friends, who were much impressed with how much Anna's health had improved. She seemed to have fresh vivacity and her youthful appearance had returned. Whilst there she attended a women's meeting and delighted everyone with her brightness and chattiness.

When they settled into Martham Vicarage in March, Anna was immediately charmed with the village which she described as 'large, with a green, and bright pleasant cottages and houses. There is work enough, with more than 1,200 souls.'

On May 4th she wrote: 'We are now getting quite established at Martham. It is so entirely not our doing, and not our particular wish, that we cannot but hope it is the appointment, for the time, of our gracious God, and that He will mercifully accept a work for Him at our hands. We are quite encouraged already, the people welcome us very heartily in our house-to-house visitation, and the Sunday and day schools are much improved. I am hoping to get up two little mothers meetings in the week, but oh, with everything any of us try to do, how entirely it is nothing without the breath from above, the breath of life. That is what we want; oh, that we may have it!'

The old Vicarage at Martham

Writing on the 24th May to the Hone family who were visiting Tirley, she said: 'I love to think of you at this sweet time of year at pretty Tirley. You are more lovely than we in Norfolk, I dare say, but I do think just now we are delicious, and D. and I think we never could live anywhere but in the country, amidst millions of primroses, bright green fields, and the delicious fruit blossoms. Perhaps, being away from them so long makes us more in rapture just now, but certainly it is a glorious season. We like our appointment here, more and more. We are able to work so pleasantly, and what we do seems appreciated, which certainly is helpful. My little mothers' meeting is quite a success; we are twenty-five, and I had thought if I got ten or twelve it would be worthwhile to go on. My second [mothers' meeting] looks hopeful also, in the little outlandish hamlet; [this could have been Cess or Damgate] but there the women are more in the fields just now. I wish I could have you all know our little abode. You would like a sight of our magnificent church; it certainly is lovely. Then the churchyard is so pleasant now, with its carpet of white and gold, perfectly covered with daisies and buttercups. My eyes have been better, but wind affects them sadly. I see I may not play any tricks with myself. Getting on so bonnily of late, I thought I might venture further and walked too far yesterday and had such a night of pain. I must go to my hamlet this afternoon.'

Anna went to her meeting, but little did she know that it was the last time she would be able to attend. The next day she had planned a visit to Lowestoft about twenty miles away but felt too unwell and was not even able to sit up for more than a few hours. Then followed days of pain and agony for which there seemed to be no relief. After a week with no sign of improvement, Anna came to the full realization that her life in this world was drawing to a close and that she must prepare for passing into the nearer presence of her Lord.

Those nursing her later said how: 'Her mind was fixed on the great change before her, and on the joy of departing to be with Christ.' The first prayer she breathed audibly was 'Wash me, and I shall be whiter than snow.' And later she asked, 'Will He forgive all my sins, and receive me?' and after a brief pause 'Yes, He died for me, that I might live.' And then the words of another hymn:

'Nothing in my hand I bring;
simply to Thy cross I cling.'

When David asked her, 'Are you happy?' she replied, 'Happy? Yes in Christ.' And then she asked him, 'Why are you so unhappy? I am so happy it is nearly finished.' And later said: 'It is sweet to die.'

In spite of extreme suffering Anna wished those around her not to be sad saying: 'Are you not glad, that I am going home, going to be with the Lord for ever?'

David, seeing her in great distress, spoke quietly the words of Charles Wesley's hymn:

'Jesu, lover of my soul,
let me to Thy bosom fly,

while the gathering waters roll,
while the tempest still is nigh:
hide me, O my Saviour, hide,
till the storm of life is past;
safe into the haven guide,
O receive my soul at last.'

That seemed to bring her solace. For some days she seemed almost unable to speak. A clergyman from a neighbouring parish came to visit on Monday 6th June and Anna managed to rouse herself and even tried to sing the hymn: 'For ever with the Lord. Amen, so let it be!'

Later she drifted into quiet peaceful sleep from which she would never awaken and at twenty to nine in the evening, in the presence of those who had lovingly cared for her, entered into her eternal rest.

A week later, on June 13th, the Revd. William Ripley presided at the burial service when Anna's mortal body was laid to rest in peace in that 'pleasant' churchyard beneath the 'carpet of white and gold, perfectly covered with daisies and buttercups.' Anna had achieved her wish – to be a martyr – but perhaps not in the way she would have remotely imagined.

The grave of Anna and David Hinderer in Martham Churchyard

# TRIBUTES

The following is the Reverend Richard Hone's tribute: 'So passed away, in her forty-fourth year, one whose health had been utterly ruined by the pestilential climate of Africa, the dangers of which she had encountered for the love of Christ. She had not held her comforts or her life dear to herself, if only she might do her Lord's work, and bring at least a few hearts to the knowledge of His name. Her desire was granted, she now rests from her labours.'

The news of Anna's death reached Ibadan on 16th July. When they had recovered from the shock of this sad news, some of those who could write sent very touching letters to David to express their sympathy and great sorrow at the passing of Anna who to them was their 'Iya' who was so greatly loved by them all. A selection from the letters in English is included here:

'The dear Iya's death took us much by surprise. Both ourselves and the Christians, for the whole week, have been deeply sorrowful. ... She has faithfully finished her course, and is now received into glory, to be for ever with her Lord and Master, whom she so faithfully served and followed. Her conjoint labours with you here, in the establishment of Christ's kingdom, upwards of sixteen years, will ever be to her praise. The sons and daughters she had kindly brought up, and cared for in the Gospel, will ever lament her loss; and her good deeds, as books, will ever be read among us. ... We are fully persuaded that you will remember the living church which God has mercifully gathered here in this place, through your instrumentality. The steady growth, and the faithful teaching in her, by your sons and daughters in the Gospel, will enable you to comfort yourself.'

'... Iya is now freed from this world of sin and sorrow for a better one, (where there is no more pain, no more trials,) to repay her labours with a crown of glory. Dear Babba, take comfort, Iya shall rise again; by this assurance only we can take comfort and be glad.'

'... It is the Lord; let Him do what seemeth Him good. In all our affliction He is afflicted and what we know not now we shall know hereafter. My whole heart bled for you, my dear Babba, for you are left alone, yet not alone, for Christ is with you. Our dear Iya, though she died, she yet speaketh. Her work in Ibadan will still live, and bear testimony of her, till such time that she will say, "These are they whom Thou hast given me." Our prayer is, though He smite may He heal, by drawing many unto His fold. We hope the dear and loving friends, who always remember us poor Africans, may still continue their love to us in the absence of Iya.'

'We are very sorry that our first letter to you is that of sympathy, and that because of our dear and loving white mother in the faith, whose face we are not privileged to see again in the body, but whose image is deeply impressed on us, and whose memory will be lasting. We deeply lament your loss and our loss, but it is the hand of our loving Father; His will must be done. Let Him do what seemeth Him good. Blessed be His Name. Our comfort is that we shall one day meet in that land where sorrow and sighing shall flee away. You both have brought Jesus with you into our town, but you have left Him among us; for this we are thankful. Having then this Jesus, and being enlightened by His Spirit, our hopes are brightened; and we mourn not, therefore, as those that have no hope. Dear Babba, we commit you, both body and soul, to the kind keeping of the great Jehovah. Mourn not your loss, for it will be joy at the last day. She is gone to her rest, and is now among the redeemed that gather around their Saviour, singing praises to His name. May we all be her boast and rejoicing at the last day. Truly her labours of love will never be forgotten among us. Let us work while it is called the day, for the night cometh when no one can work. And may we walk in faith that we may meet where we shall part no more!

We remain, dear Babba,

Your sympathizing sons and daughters in the faith,

THE IBADAN CHURCH MEMBERS'

# POSTSCRIPT

DAVID HINDERER served the Church at Martham as Assistant Curate until 1873. After Anna's death, her step-sister Sarah Georgina Martin became housekeeper for him at the Vicarage there. During his time in Martham his health improved considerably, so that eventually he was deemed by the CMS to be fit enough to return to missionary work. In 1874 he returned to the Yoruba Country of West Africa. He established missions at Lekki and Ode Ondo in the coastal region near to Lagos. On visiting Ibadan he was delighted to see the continuing steady progress of the work he had started there and the strong witness of the Christian congregations. In 1877 he retired from missionary work in Africa. He was appointed assistant curate at Hatherden, Hampshire in 1878 where he stayed for several years until final retirement. When he was no longer fit enough to work he spent his time translating books and hymns into Yoruba.

He was financially supported by the money that he should have received as an allowance in the years when he was cut off in Ibadan. It had been returned to England and invested on his behalf, so was available to him when he needed it in later life.

He spent some time in Germany and Switzerland but eventually returned to England, to live at Westbourne in Bournemouth. Anna's step-sister Sarah cared for him during his years of increasing infirmity until he died on the 16th September 1890. He was finally laid to rest with Anna in Martham Churchyard.

DANIEL OLUBI took charge of the Kudeti Mission when David Hinderer returned to England in 1869. He was ordained a deacon in 1871 and a priest in 1876. The rest of his life was spent in the service of the Church at Ibadan. When he died in 1912 at the age of 82 he was laid to rest in the churchyard at St. David's Church, Kudeti.

THE REV. D. OLUBI,
*C.M.S. Native Pastor at Ibadan, Yoruba Mission.*
*Ordained* 1871.

MRS. DOLAPO FALOMO, who recently retired from her post as the Principal of St. Anne's School and was once a pupil there, wrote, 'I am happy to let you know that Anna Hinderer is very much remembered in Ibadan. Two schools were established through them. St. Anne's School, Molete, Ibadan was said to have been named in her memory.

Two stained glass windows are in her honour, one in the old St. Anne's School Chapel (now part of the new church) and the other in the new large church, both just across the road from St. Anne's School, Molete.

The Church recently started another school named St. Anne's Comprehensive College, Ibadan.

Also Yejide Girls Grammar School, Kudeti was named after one of her adopted daughters whose name was Yejide. [Yejide was a daughter of Chief Olumloyo and one of the first children to join the school at the Kudeti Mission.]

The Old Kudeti House is still standing at St. David's Cathedral, Kudeti, also named after David Hinderer. It is an old valued monument which cannot be destroyed.

The name Anna Hinderer is very much valued.'

# THE PEOPLE MENTIONED IN THE STORY

Revd. Richard Hone – Rector of Halesowen, a friend of Anna and David Hinderer. His daughters compiled the first book about Anna - 'Seventeen Years in the Yoruba Country'- and he wrote the introduction
Revd. David Hinderer – Anna's husband
William and Margaret (née Woodroffe) Martin – Anna's parents
William Woodroffe Martin – Anna's brother
Charles Edward Martin – Anna's half-brother
John Martin – Anna's grandfather
Mary Martin – Anna's aunt
Revd. Francis Cunningham – Vicar of Lowestoft
Richenda Cunningham née Gurney – the wife of Francis Cunningham
Hannah - Lady Buxton – widow of Sir Thomas Fowell Buxton and sister of Richenda Cunningham

*These people sailed on the *S.S. Propontis* with Anna and David.
*Revd. J. Theophilus Kefer – went to the Ibadan Mission with David and Anna
*The Right Revd. Owen Vidal and Mrs Vidal – the first bishop of Sierra Leone and his wife.
*The Revd. Richard and Mrs Paley – went to serve at Abeokuta Mission
*Mr Hensman – a medical missionary who died at Abeokuta in 1853
*Mr Gerst – went to serve at Lagos Mission
*Mr John Andrew Maser – went to serve at Abeokuta Mission and later at Lagos
Revd. Charles Andrew Gollmer and Mrs Gollmer – missionaries at the Lagos Mission
Revd. Samuel Crowther – a freed slave who became Bishop of the Niger
Daniel Olubi – from Abeokuta. Anna and David's great and valued African friend and colleague

Susanna – Anna's maid who married Daniel Olubi
Daniel, Jonathan, Bertha and Tilda Olubi – the children of Daniel and Susanna Olubi
Olumloyo – one of the chiefs of Ibadan and the father of Akielle and Yejide. He was killed in battle in 1857.
Simon, Jacob, Benjamin and Odehinde – African menservants and workers at Ibadan Mission
Martha – the ten year old daughter of an unnamed Christian visitor
Revd. Henry and Mrs Townsend – missionaries at Abeokuta
Laniyono, Adelothan and Abudo – boys who attended the mission school
Mrs Selina Clemens – the schoolmistress at Charlotte, Sierra Leone
Revd. William Augustin Bernard Johnson - 'Massa' Johnson served at Sierra Leone from 1816 to 1823
Bale – the head chief at Ibadan
Revd. Ulrich Graf – the Archdeacon of Sierra Leone from 1853
Dr Irving – explorer and plantsman
King of the Ijebu – visited by David and Dr. Irving
The black Iyalode of Ibadan - possibly named Efusetan Aniwura
Onisaga, Akielle, Lanyino, Arubo, Elukolo, Ogunyomi, Mary Ann Macauley – children baptised in 1855
Revd. Gottlieb Frederick Buhler – a missionary at Abeokuta who helped at Ibadan 1855 - 56 while David and Anna were on their first furlough
Revd. James Jonathan Hoch – a missionary at Ibadan 1855 -56
Revd. Joseph Smith and his wife Ellen. They took charge of the Ibadan Mission 1862 - 63 when Anna and David were on their second furlough.
Revd. Adolphus Christian Mann – a missionary at Ijaye
Lieutenant Dolben – rescued the missionaries from Ijaye before the town was destroyed
Revd. Edward Roper – from Ijaye. An evangelist who joined the Ibadan Mission and served at Ogunpo. He was later ordained.
Konigbagbe – the girl who came from Oyo and became Anna's personal maid
Henry Johnson – the catechist who moved to Ibadan from Sierra Leone with his wife and six surviving children to serve at the Ogunpa Mission Station. He died on the 10th February 1865 and

was buried in the churchyard at Kudeti. Of his four sons who grew to adulthood, three became priests and one became a doctor. They all became leading figures in the Christian life of the communities in which they lived.

William Allen – the catechist who moved from Sierra Leone and served at the Aremo Mission Station

James Berber – a Yoruba native catechist who died very suddenly in 1858.

Ogunyomi – the girl who was reunited with her mother Lucy Fagbeade

Lucy Fagbeade – the mother of Ogunyomi. She became the cook at the mission

Arubo – a boy who was rescued from starvation and lived for 11 years but died in 1865

Sophie Ajele – taken into the mission by one of the catechists as her mother wanted to sell her

Durojula – a girl who went with Anna to Lagos in 1859

Charles Buxton – son of Sir Thomas and Lady Hannah Fowell Buxton. He sent boxes of tools to the Mission

George Jeffries – a CMS lay evangelist who joined the Ibadan Mission in 1860

King of Dahomey – invaded Abeokuta in 1860

Odeheinde (or Okuseinde) – he was the servant who looked after the horses at the Mission. He later became a catechist and scripture reader and served at the Ogunpa Mission Station

Balogum Olumloyo – a friend they met on the way to Ijaye

Revd. William Nottidge Ripley – assistant curate at Lowestoft, later Vicar of St Giles Church, Norwich. He married Laura Gurney, the widow of John Gurney. The Ripley family lived at Earlham Hall.

The Right Revd. John Bowen – 3rd Bishop of Sierra Leone

Eyila – the baby girl rescued in 1864

Bashorun – the head chief of Ibadan who died in 1867

Antonio – a former slave who lived in the Kudeti compound for 10 years

Talabi - the daughter of Antonio. She had a son aged two.

Samuel – a young boy who was determined to be baptised

Samuel Johnson – became the schoolmaster at Ibadan. He was a son of Henry, the catechist from Sierra Leone. He later became a priest and wrote *The History of the Yorubas*.
Oyebode – one of the boys who was given special lessons by Anna. He was with her on her last journey to Lagos. Later he became the schoolmaster at the Aremo Mission Station.
Mr. and Mrs. Mather – the residents of Bootle Hall near Liverpool
Mr and Mrs George Head Head – of Rickerby House, Carlisle
Sarah Head Head was a daughter of Samuel Gurney (the banker) and a niece of Richenda Cunningham.
The Reverend George Pearse – Vicar of Martham from 1834 to 1876. He was the father of Laura Ripley.

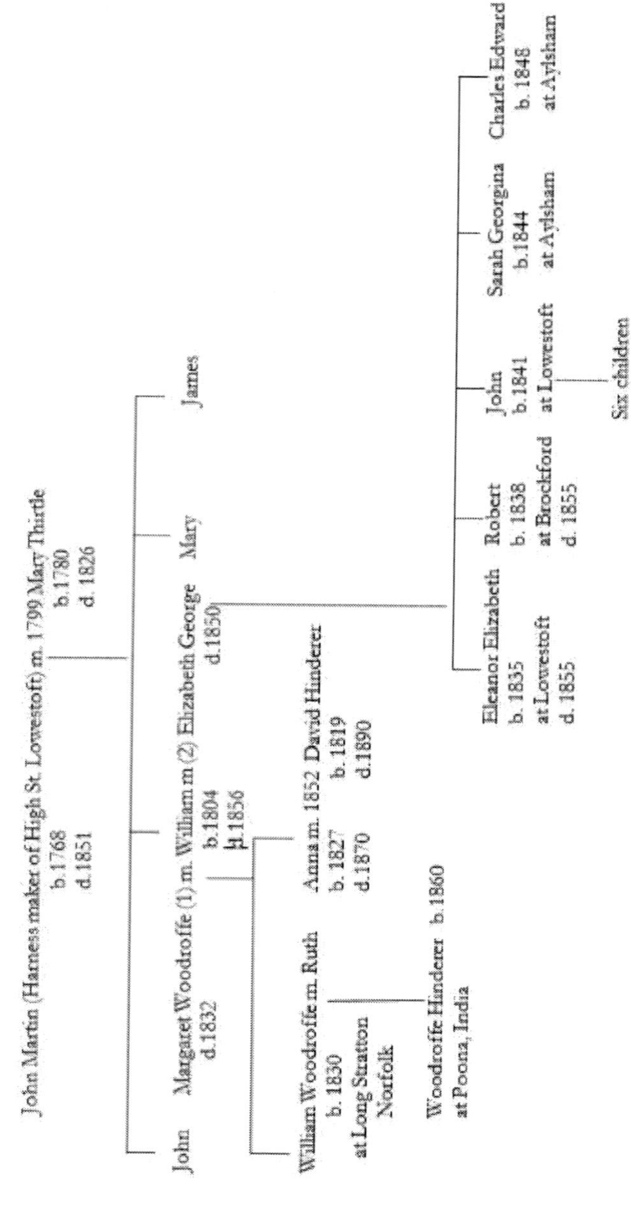
THE MARTIN FAMILY TREE
John Martin (Harness maker of High St. Lowestoft) m. 1799 Mary Thirtle
b.1768
d.1851
b.1780
d. 1826
John
Margaret Woodroffe (1) m. William m (2) Elizabeth George
d.1832
b.1804
d.1856
d.1850
Mary
James
William Woodroffe m. Ruth
b. 1830
at Long Stratton
Norfolk
Woodroffe Hinderer b.1860
at Poona, India
Anna m. 1852 David Hinderer
b. 1827
d.1870
b. 1819
d.1890
Eleanor Elizabeth
b. 1835
at Lowestoft
d. 1855
Robert
b. 1838
at Brockford
d. 1855
John
b.1841
at Lowestoft
Six children
Sarah Georgina
b.1844
at Aylsham
Charles Edward
b. 1848
at Aylsham

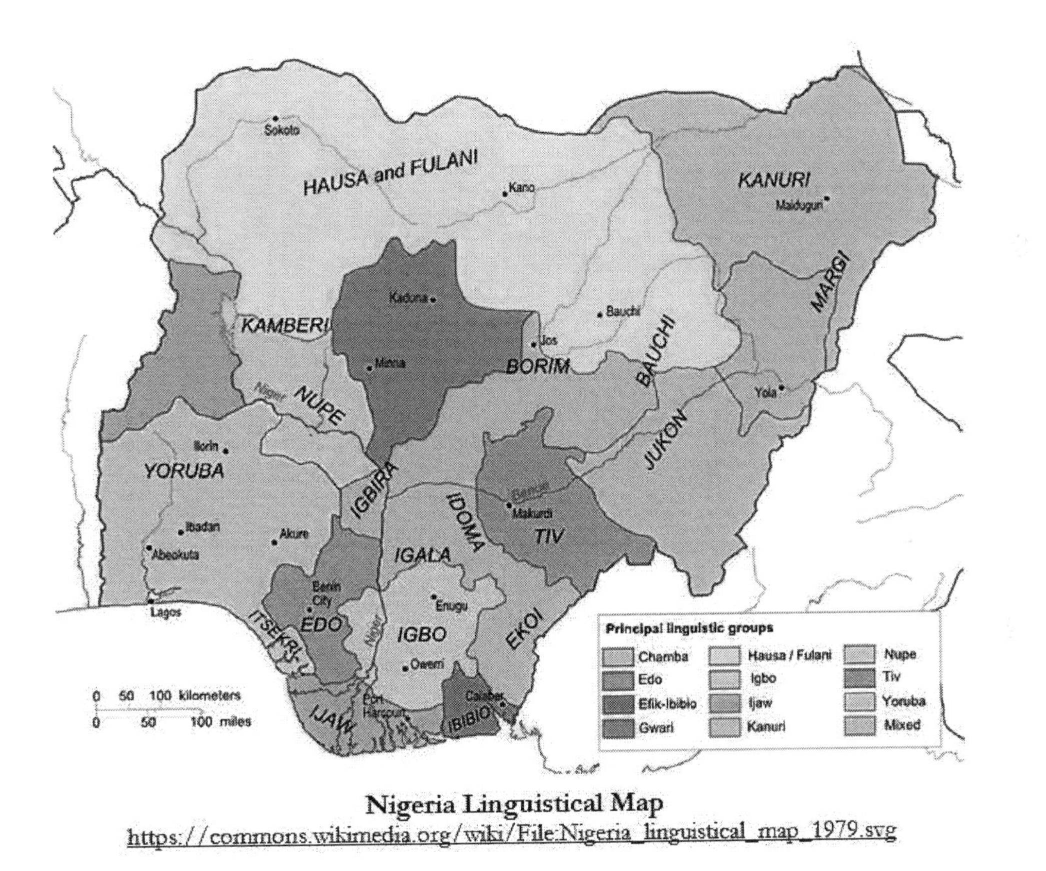


**Nigeria Linguistical Map**

https://commons.wikimedia.org/wiki/File:Nigeria_linguistical_map_1979.svg

# SOURCES OF INFORMATION

## General

Correspondence from Mrs Anna Hinderer and Rev David Hinderer to Mr J. Frazer, Esquire of Lowestoft, Nov 1864, re death and bequests of Rev Cunningham.
Lowestoft Record Office - reference 332/3/15.

Correspondence relating to Church Management.
Lowestoft Record Office - reference 332/2/20-31 and 332/3/1-16.

Church Missionary Society Archives. Birmingham University Library, Birmingham.

*Dictionary of African Christian Biography* (website).
http://www.dacb.org

Nigeria Linguistical Map
https://commons.wikimedia.org/wiki/File:Nigeria_linguistical_map_1979.svg

## Books

BUXTON E. Ellen. (Ellen R. C. Creighton, Ed.) *Family Sketchbook a Hundred Years Ago*. 1969.

*Crockford's Clerical Directories.* Church House Publishing.

FALOLA Toyin.

a. Efusetan Aniwura of Ibadan (1820s – 1874) - A Woman Who Rose to the Rank of a Chief but whom Male Rivals Destroyed.
b. Samuel Johnson (1840-1901) and the History of the Yorubas.
   Chapters 2 & 5 in *The Human Tradition in Modern Africa* by Dennis D. Cordell. Rowman & Littlefield Publishers. 2012.

HARE Augustus J.C. *The Gurneys of Earlham*. G. Allen, London. 1895.

HONE C.A. and D. *Seventeen Years In The Yoruba Country.* Religious Tract Society, London. 1877. Available online from the Robarts Library of the University of Toronto. https://archive.org/details/yorubacountry00hinduoft

STOCK Eugene. *The History Of The Church Missionary Society Its Environment Its Men And Its Work.* Church Missionary Society, London. 1899.

## ABOUT THE AUTHOR

Ann Meakin (née Baldwin) grew up in the London suburb of North Wembley where she was a member of St Cuthbert's Church. She was educated at Harrow County School for Girls. In 1965 Ann moved to Martham with her first husband, Alan Bridges. She became a member of Martham Parish Church and has played the organ for services there since 1978. Several years after Alan's death, Ann married John Meakin and also acquired three wonderful step-children.

Following retirement after many years in the Civil Service, Ann was able to pursue her interest in local history by enrolling in an Extramural Studies course at the University of East Anglia under the renowned J. C. (Chris) Barringer. This has enabled her to study a great many aspects of the history of Martham. She has published two books and has co-written several other publications. Ann is a co-founder of the Martham Local History Group and is currently its president.

Ann at Anna and David Hinderer's grave.
Photograph by Michael Vickers